Laura Veenema

MODERN
Improv Quilting

BE THE BOSS OF YOUR DESIGN
TECHNIQUES & PROJECTS TO GET YOU STARTED

stash BOOKS

an imprint of C&T Publishing

Text copyright © 2024 by Laura Veenema

Styled photography and artwork copyright © 2024 by C&T Publishing, Inc.

How-to photography copyright © 2024 by Laura Veenema

PUBLISHER: Amy Barrett-Daffin

CREATIVE DIRECTOR: Gailen Runge

SENIOR EDITOR: Roxane Cerda

EDITOR: Madison Moore

TECHNICAL EDITOR: Del Walker, Debbie Rodgers

COVER/BOOK DESIGNER: April Mostek

PRODUCTION COORDINATOR: Tim Manibusan

ILLUSTRATOR: Aliza Shalit, Tim Manibusan

PHOTOGRAPHY COORDINATOR: Rachel Ackley

FRONT COVER PHOTOGRAPHY by Kate Faber

STYLED PHOTOGRAPHY by Kate Faber, unless otherwise noted

HOW-TO PHOTOGRAPHY by Laura Veenema

Published by Stash Books, an imprint of C&T Publishing, Inc., P.O. Box 1456, Lafayette, CA 94549

Library of Congress Cataloging-in-Publication Data

Names: Veenema, Laura Kay, 1986- author.

Title: Modern improv quilting : be the boss of your design; techniques & projects to get you started / Laura Veenema.

Description: Lafayette, CA : Stash Books, an imprint of C&T Publishing, Inc., [2024] | Summary: "Modern Improv Quilting is an introduction to, guide through, and reflection on creating quilts and quilted projects that will never be made exactly the same way twice. Laura introduces readers to her methods for choosing fresh color, shape, and function, and walks them through quilt, home, and accessory projects"-- Provided by publisher.

Identifiers: LCCN 2024005959 | ISBN 9781644034620 (trade paperback) | ISBN 9781644034637 (ebook)

Subjects: LCSH: Quilting--Patterns. | Patchwork--Patterns. | Patchwork quilts. | BISAC: CRAFTS & HOBBIES / Quilts & Quilting | CRAFTS & HOBBIES / Sewing

Classification: LCC TT835 .V44 2024 | DDC 746.46--dc23/ eng/20240310

LC record available at https://lccn.loc.gov/2024005959

Printed in the USA

10 9 8 7 6 5 4 3 2

DEDICATION

For Matthew, Caleb, Luke and Violet. You are our most beautiful masterpieces.

ACKNOWLEDGMENTS

Writing a quilting book is, quite literally, a dream come true for me. What an incredible gift this process has been—even better than in my imaginings. It would not have been possible without a village of people helping me. Thank you all, so much.

I want to acknowledge and thank my beautiful little family, my first and best dream-come-true. Matthew, you lead the way for your siblings with your selflessness, thoughtfulness and adventurism. Caleb, your creativity, kindness, and sensitivity are your superpowers. Luke, your energy, joy and incredible courage (born from diabetic adversity) inspire me to do hard things (like writing a book.) Finally, our strong and smart Violet: you are the gift we didn't know we needed. Thank you for taking long naps so I could write. Thank you, sweet kiddos, for being you—each individual masterpieces. I cannot wait to see how you change the world.

Our big and busy family juggles a lot, and Jeremy's unflappability and selflessness deserves the credit for keeping us all steady. Thank you, my love, for all the time and energy you've invested and sacrificed in order to help achieve this quilting and book-writing dream. Thank you for your good humor and constant encouragement and irrepressible kindness. I love you. You'll always be my favorite.

I want to acknowledge everyone who helped care for these sweet babies so I could write and quilt. Our babysitters and friends. Their teachers and coaches. Grandpa Bob and Grandma Heidi. We have the world's best village.

Thank you, too, to all of the women who contributed to the quilts and images in this book. Thank you, Molly Kohler and Janet Hollandsworth—long-arm machinist extraordinaires. Thank you to Kate Faber—the most generous photographer and friend. Thank you Amy Heitman and Brynn Jensen and Kate Neckers. Your eye for beauty brings joy to the world. Thank you to my cutting counter friends at Field Fabrics. Your encouragement bolsters me every time I see you. Not one of you is a Brenda.

I want to acknowledge my brilliant and patient editor, Madison Moore. Thank you for believing in me and for making this whole book happen.

I want to thank Mary Van Loh, my quilting mentor. Your gentle teaching, your life-giving encouragement, and your selfless hospitality quite literally changed the course of my life. Thank you, too, to Pastor Rog Nelson and my friends at Hope CRC. When I think of my learning to quilt, I think of you all.

I want to recognize the friends who, throughout both business building and book writing, have told me that I am *capable* (something I think we all need to be reminded of, once in a while.) There are too many to thank, but I think particularly of Rachel, Todd, Kellynne, Emily, Jill, Ali, Caroline, Lauren, Anne, and my sister Stephanie. I think of Emily, Sarah, Dana, Emily, and Emalyn. I think of Brian and Virginia, Kyle and Allie, Taylor and Annie. And my parents, Jan and Steve—thank you for your **You Can** legacy of encouragement, optimism, and hope. I love you so. The unfaltering support of all of you—and countless others—continues to be the wind at my back.

Thanks be to God, too. Thank you for a sewing community and a book contract and nimble hands. Thank you for the earth that grows cotton, the farmers who harvest it, and the artisans who make it into fabric. Thank you for the way you create wholeness out of broken pieces, again and again and again. Thank you for Jesus and his radical and atoning self-sacrifice for the sake of restoration. Thank you for your love that will not let me go—it gives me strength for today and bright hope for tomorrow. It is Christ alone who has given me this new song. To Him be the glory.

May the beauty of quilts remind the world that all hope is not yet lost.

Contents

Improv Quilting For the Win

I've always hated following quilt patterns because I always worry that I'm not doing it *right*. What if my seams don't line up? And what page was I on? And oops, my quilt definitely doesn't match the picture. But with improvisational quilting, I can just quilt—because there is no *right* or *wrong*.

I've heard that when marathon runners get in the zone running they feel a *runner's high*. (I think they are actually all making that up because running is objectively terrible, and no one actually enjoys running.) But, I have the same experience with improv quilting. When I am in the zone—when I have caught the improv wave for a specific quilt—I feel a height of creative emotion that just takes over.

I also get a thrill of power. With improv quilting, the pattern is not the boss; I am the boss. I have control over the design, color, form, function and future of this one, tiny thing. And that doesn't feel so tiny, does it? It feels beautiful. It feels like energy to surrender all of the other tiny and not-so-tiny things that I can't control throughout my day because, at least with this quilt, what I say goes.

The three improvisational quilting techniques taught in this book are designed to get you started with some basic blocks, and then let you catch your own improv wave. I hope that once you have the hang of the different shapes involved in each technique, you can just quilt. Maybe you'll love it so much you'll get your own quilting high. (If not, you can always try running?)

In addition to those technique chapters, I've included several projects for making specific quilts and other goods that use those improv techniques. Whether you want a lot of guidance or a little, this book will help you get started on your own modern improv quilting journey.

I hope that besides the quilting guidance, this book also brings you joy. I hope improv quilting lifts you outside of yourself for just a little bit. I hope this book reminds you that there is still beauty in the world and hope to be found, even if it is just in the comfort of a quilt. Share your quilts with **#modernimprovquilting**

Materials and Tools

LET'S TALK FABRIC

QUALITY MATTERS

My quilting mentor advised me early on to be choosy about fabric quality. She told me that the very inexpensive quilting cotton doesn't have a tight warp and weft. Practically, I have found this to be true. The higher the quality of fabrics, the easier they are to sew. My favorite solid non-organic quilting cottons are Robert Kaufman Kona cottons.

SUSTAINABILITY MATTERS

For ease in writing this book, I defaulted to using the non-organic quilting cotton that is easy to find and relatively inexpensive to purchase because I know organic fabrics are neither cheap nor ubiquitous. But I do think organic fabrics, and specifically those certified with the Global Organic Textile Standard (GOTS) are worth serious consideration. Having the GOTS-certification means that the production of that fabric passed scrutiny in regards to both its environmental impact (to reduce toxic pesticides) and its treatment of workers (to reduce exploitation.)

It is also worth checking for an OEKO-TEX label on fabrics (water-resistant fabrics, specifically, for our purposes in this book). OEKO-TEX tests for the presence of over 350 toxic chemicals in fabrics, so certification means that harmful chemicals won't be a problem in the fabric we are using. This matters. Our planet matters, and people matter. If the end goal of quilting is to bring a little bit more beauty to the world, then it would make sense to eliminate as much ugliness from the growing, processing, and production of that fabric as possible.

Another way to quilt more sustainably is to use linen fabric. Did you know that linen uses four times less water to grow than cotton does? I love using linen fabric alongside quilting cotton—especially for the backing of my quilts.

Another sustainable quilting practice is to look at local resale shops for quilting fabric. Buying second hand fabric saves it from ending up in the landfill and reduces the need for more fabric production. Shopping locally also reduces the fossil fuels needed to transport goods from place to place.

THE QUILTY GUTS

BATTING

Different types of batting (the material that is sandwiched between the top and backing of the quilt) have different benefits.

My favorite is wool batting. Wool is breathable but warm and usually has a high loft, which means it is fluffy and thick. This makes the quilting pattern more defined and the quilt itself hearty. Wool batting can be expensive, though.

My second favorite type of batting is bamboo, a natural fiber that is breathable and strong. Bamboo also has antimicrobial properties, which means it resists mold and mildew. Interestingly, growing bamboo requires only a third of the water that cotton needs, which means it is better for the planet. Bamboo is also grown without pesticides and is self-regenerating, so it doesn't need to be planted again year after year. But, bamboo batting is also not cheap.

Another natural option is cotton batting. I use cotton batting when I need a breathable quilt that has that flat, traditional look. Its low loft makes it easy to work with, and it is less expensive than wool batting.

Polyester batting is a cheaper, more lightweight option, but I don't recommend it. If the polyester batting gets too hot (like with a hot iron), it could actually melt. Polyester batting is also prone to bearding. Bearding is when little tufts of the batting poke through the holes where the quilting pattern was stitched in.

THREAD

My best advice for beginning quilters: choose a light-colored, natural cotton thread. My favorite is Gutermann 100% cotton. I use that thread for all of my piecing. I find it strong and durable (no thread wax needed) but easy to control.

ESSENTIAL TOOLS AND EQUIPMENT

SHARP, HOT, POKEY THINGS

Quilting requires a variety of sharp, hot, pokey things:

- Sharp, fabric-specific scissors: I like Kai N5220.
- Rotary cutter and blades: I suggest Olfa 60mm.
- Safety gloves: I suggest these if you're new to rotary cutting or accident prone.
- Cutting mat: I suggest Fiskars 24˝ × 36˝.
- Acrylic quilting ruler: I mainly use a 6˝ × 24˝ ruler.
- Pressing iron: Go dust her off and give her a kiss because she's going to be your new best friend! I use a high-quality Chi Iron.
- Ironing board or mat: I suggest a wool pressing mat because it's not bulky.
- Sewing machine needles: I recommend Schmetz 80/12.
- Marking tool: I use a hera marker or water-soluble pen/pencil.
- Seam ripper: Let her live right next to the sewing machine. She'll be ready to come to your rescue.
- Straight pins with flat heads for piecing fabric
- Big curved safety pins for sandwiching the quilt layers
- Plastic mini sewing clamps

MECHANICAL THINGS

There are some people who like to hand piece and hand stitch their quilts. These are the same people, I think, who churn their own butter and drink bone broth and like to mention they don't own a TV. If you are one of these people, God bless you and your delicious butter. But if you are not, you'll need a sewing machine.

The best sewing machine for a beginner quilter is usually the free sewing machine. So if your aunt has one you can borrow, go for it. If you're ready to purchase your own and want one that will last, I recommend splurging on a Bernina. To be sure, buying a high-quality sewing machine is an investment, but making that investment will save you from throwing good money after bad. My BFF Bernie has not broken once in eight years of daily use. She is a patient companion and a reliable colleague. (I am now realizing I may need to get out more.)

Anytime you're ready to sew, you will need the following list of tools:

Tools and Materials for Every Project

Rotary cutter

Cutting mat

Scissors

Acrylic ruler

Sewing machine and needle

Cotton thread

Hera marker or water-soluble marker

Straight pins

Walking foot

Iron/ironing board

TEMPLATES

To help cut curved shapes, templates are provided as downloads accessed via a QR code. You'll want to print the templates out on paper, (cardstock is ideal) then use scissors to cut them out. Place the template on the fabric and use a water soluble marker to trace around the cut-out template. Finally, use fabric scissors or a rotary cutter to cut the curved piece out of the fabric.

To access the templates needed for the blocks and projects, scan this QR code or go to tinyurl.com/11573-patterns-download

Color and Balance

COLOR

I had a friend named Nora in elementary school. We were Nora and Laura. We'd use embroidery floss to create friendship bracelets and try to sell them from a lemonade stand. I remember one day, as I paired brown and lime green threads, I concluded that the best color combinations didn't actually match. That was the beginning of what would become a passion for unorthodox color exploration.

Nowadays, I stand in front of the fabric wall at the fabric store and think, "How can I make cutting-counter-Brenda clutch her pearls today?" Then I bring my stack of fabrics to the counter where Brenda sniffs, "Oh. This selection is *interesting*." (Read: she hates it.) Well Brenda, I wouldn't pick the puffy paint, cat-in-a-basket sweater you're wearing either, so *to each their own.*

SOME COLOR SUGGESTIONS

This is a universal truth and there is no escaping it: red and black look bad together. So do purple and yellow. This truth also goes for blue and gold. Here's a rule of thumb: if the colors you are choosing for a quilt belong on the uniform of a professional basketball player, they look bad together.

Brown and pink, though? That's a winning combination. There is something *softer*, to me, about brown and pink than black and red or yellow and purple. The difference lies in the colors' locations on the color wheel.

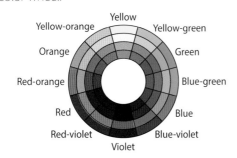

Brown is a shade of orange—orange with black added. Pink is a tint of red—pink with white added. Orange and red sit near to each other on the color wheel, so they play nicely with each other. Therefore their offspring, brown and pink, will also play nicely together.

Traditional color advice says that complementary colors—colors on opposite ends of the color wheel—make good pairs. So, according to this logic, purple and yellow are beautiful friends. I, however, say **no thank you**!

Here are my *guiding* principles for color choosing, though I do break my own rules:

1. Stay away from a quilt that consists of only classic crayon colors. Look for tints, tones, and shades of those colors instead.

2. Combine both the shade and tint of one color, like Cinnamon Red and Coral Red. They don't "match," but they compliment each other so well.

3. When using many hues for one quilt, stay on one half of the color wheel. So maybe in addition to Cinnamon Red and Coral Red, add: Teal, Copen Blue, Foxglove Pink, and Lingerie Pink.

4. If you want a pastel quilt, use all tints. If you want a moody quilt, use all shades. If you want an *interesting* quilt use a combination of tints, shades and pure colors. But keep it balanced. If you only use one really light pastel tint with six moody shades, the pastel might stick out like a sore thumb.

USING WHITE IN A QUILT

Here is another universal truth: white fabric gets dirty. There is no getting around it. And who wants a dirty quilt?! Well, me! I do! I want a dirty quilt! My quilts want to be dirty, too. Because clean and pristine quilts don't get snuggled by tiny sticky hands. Clean quilts don't get schlepped through the dusty paths of the park in search of the perfect picnic spot. Dirty quilts, though, are cherished and known and loved for years. So go ahead and use white and get it dirty, too!

CHOOSING A BACKING FABRIC

In this book, you will seldom see printed fabrics on the front of a quilt, but having a modern patterned backing fabric can add a fun layer of visual texture to your quilt. I like Ruby Star Society and Kelly Ventura patterned fabrics. Typically, though, I choose solid-color backing fabric—oftentimes linen—that compliments the colors in the quilt.

BALANCE

One of the biggest obstacles to improv quilting is making the quilt look *cohesive* instead of *messy*.

BALANCE OF SHAPE AND SCALE

What is the first shape your eyes are drawn to when you look at an improv quilt? It will probably be whatever shape is holding the most weight. Maybe that is the *biggest* shape, or the shape that *repeats* the most frequently. It might also be the shape that is the most notoriously quilty: the square. I recommend using squares sparingly. Giant and tiny shapes can also be attention hogs. Any shape whose size is vastly different from its surrounding shapes will be noticed right away. In the technique chapters, I've given example measurements for shapes that are balanced in size. If you want to create bigger or smaller shapes, go for it! But, scale *all* of the shapes proportionally.

THE SPIDERWEB CHECK

All of your colors and shapes should be spread evenly throughout the quilt top. Avoid having one color pooled in a corner or all of one shape crowded into the same quadrant.

One way to check for balance is to draw an imaginary spider web. First, lay all of the "blocks" on the floor as you plan to combine them. Next, find a chair to stand (safely) on. Look down at the blocks and find all of the places where one color is used—let's say teal. In your mind, draw an imaginary web between all of the teal shapes. Your web should stretch over and across your quilt. If your web is just on one side, in one corner, or imbalanced, move your blocks around and try again. Repeat that imaginary web-drawing for all of the colors and all of the shapes in the quilt.

How to Make a Quilt

Though this book focuses on piecing, there are also some basic steps you'll need to follow to make every quilt. For all piecing, use a ¼˝ seam. There is also no need to backstitch, as crossing seam lines will anchor each other. Yardages and instructions are based on 42˝ of usable width.

CUTTING FABRIC

I use some consistent methods that make cutting easier. Start by folding the yardage for a color in half, selvage to selvage. Then, for efficient cutting when you need the same shape from multiple colors, layer 2 colors on top of one another, aligning their selvages. I always like to have the selvage edge of my folded fabric on the left side of the cutting mat and the folded edge on the right side of the cutting mat.

Using a quilting ruler and rotary cutter, trim the top edges off to create a crisp top line. Then, do the same thing to trim the selvages off of the left side. You're now ready to cut the shapes you need!

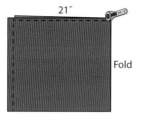

I start most projects by cutting strips that are a specific width × WOF (width of fabric). For example, to cut a 2″ × WOF strip, measure 2″ down from the top of the fabric. Then, cut horizontally to make a strip (folded in half). From there, follow the instructions to subcut the strips as needed, or use them for assembly.

PREPARING THE QUILT SANDWICH

A quilt sandwich consists of a pieced quilt top, batting, and a layer of backing fabric on the bottom.

READY THE QUILT TOP

Press all the seams as flat as possible, but don't over-iron and distort the shapes. You should also square the quilt—trim it to make sure the corners are 90° and the parallel sides are the same length. Measure across the length and width at several points, trimming each whole side to be even with the shortest measurement.

READY THE BATTING AND BACK

Cut the batting and backing to be approximately 4″ larger than the quilt top on all sides. You will likely need to piece together fabric for the backing.

SQUASH AND BASTE

Lay the backing fabric wrong-side up and tape the edges down on the floor with masking tape. Center the batting on top, smoothing and squashing out any folds and wrinkles. Then, place the quilt top right side up on top of the batting and backing, making sure it is also centered. Smooth and squash that layer out, too.

Basting keeps the quilt layers from shifting while you are quilting. You can baste with an adhesive spray or by using quilting pins placed about a fist's width apart. Begin basting in the center and move toward the edges. Try not to pin directly on the lines where you intend to quilt.

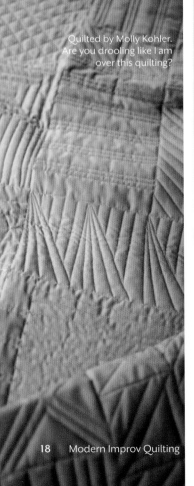

Quilted by Molly Kohler. Are you drooling like I am over this quilting?

QUILT THAT BABY!

Quilting enhances the pieced design of the quilt, and there are endless ways to do it. You may choose to quilt-in-the-ditch, echo the pieced shapes, use straight horizontal or vertical lines, or do your own free-motion quilting. You get to decide! Remember to check your batting manufacturer's recommendations for how close the quilting lines must be.

If quilting isn't something you feel up for, you can also hire someone else to do it. Your local quilt shop can help you find someone who offers long-arm machine services. Send them your quilt top and backing, and they will do the rest!

BIND THE EDGES

Trim the excess batting and backing to make it even with the edges of the quilt top. Cut binding strips 2½" wide and as long as possible. Piece them together with diagonal seams to make a continuous binding strip that is as long as the perimeter of the quilt plus about 5". Trim the small diagonal seam allowances to ¼" and press them open.

Press the entire strip in half lengthwise with wrong sides together. With raw edges even, pin the binding to the back edge of the quilt about a foot away from one of the corners, leaving the first 6" of the binding unattached. Sew from the first pin until right before the next corner, using a ¼" seam allowance.

Stop ¼" away from the first corner (see Fig. A), and backstitch one stitch. Lift the presser foot and needle. Rotate the quilt one-quarter turn. Fold the binding at a right angle so it extends straight above the quilt and the fold forms a 45° angle in the corner (see Fig. B). Then bring the binding strip down even with the edge of the quilt (see Fig. C). Begin sewing at the folded edge. Repeat at all corners.

Continue stitching until you are 2" from the beginning of the binding strip.

FINISH THE BINDING

After stitching around the quilt, fold the end tail of the binding strip where it meets the beginning tail and trim, leaving 2⅛" beyond the fold (see Fig. D).

Fold the raw edge of the beginning tail in about ½" and place the end tail of the binding strip over the folded beginning tail, overlapping them by about 1½". Stitch from the point you stopped, over the overlap, and slightly beyond the starting stitches.

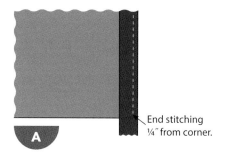

End stitching ¼" from corner.

A

First fold

B

Second fold

C

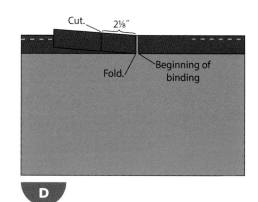

Cut.　2⅛"

Beginning of binding

Fold.

D

Mitered corner

TURN AND SEW

Fold the binding over the raw edges to the quilt front, and press down, tucking and pressing the folded corners to create a mitered look. Use clips to secure the binding as needed. Traditionally, you would now hand-stitch to invisibly attach the binding. But, instead, I machine stitch that binding so securely that it could be machine washed from here until eternity and not pop a stitch.

To do this, slowly and carefully remove sewing clips as you run the quilt binding through the machine, with the quilt facing right-side up. Try to get the stitches as close to the folded edge of the binding as possible. As you go, stitch carefully to hold the folded the corners in place, and backstitch every time you start and stop sewing the binding.

Color Chart

This book uses a consistent color naming system that is based on Kona Quilting Cotton colors. See all colors, along with the abbreviations used in this book, below. There's one exception: color HH is an Art Gallery Fabrics design.

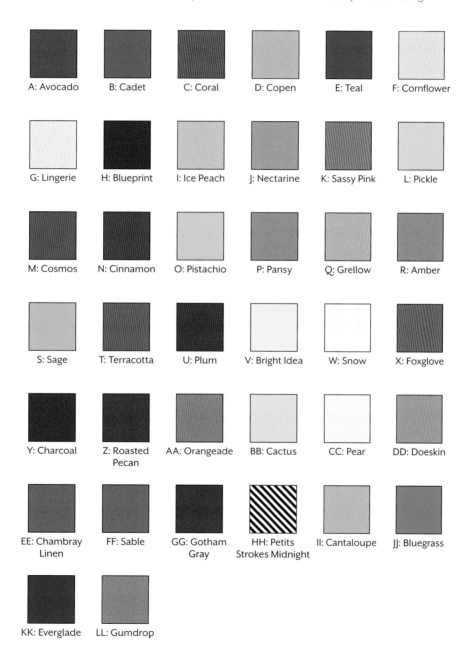

A: Avocado B: Cadet C: Coral D: Copen E: Teal F: Cornflower

G: Lingerie H: Blueprint I: Ice Peach J: Nectarine K: Sassy Pink L: Pickle

M: Cosmos N: Cinnamon O: Pistachio P: Pansy Q: Grellow R: Amber

S: Sage T: Terracotta U: Plum V: Bright Idea W: Snow X: Foxglove

Y: Charcoal Z: Roasted Pecan AA: Orangeade BB: Cactus CC: Pear DD: Doeskin

EE: Chambray Linen FF: Sable GG: Gotham Gray HH: Petits Strokes Midnight II: Cantaloupe JJ: Bluegrass

KK: Everglade LL: Gumdrop

Classic Easy Improv

Technique 1 sample quilt layout

FINAL DIMENSIONS: 60˝ × 53˝

This first type of improv technique is straightforward but impressive. A few basic geometric shapes pieced in simple but intentional ways make it look like you had the design planned all along. In this chapter, you'll learn how to cut and assemble the basic "blocks" of this technique, and also how to add variations to make it all your own.

This technique is used to make A Quilt to Impress Your Mother-In-Law (page 82) and The (Not-Boring) Neutral Quilt (page 96).

CHOOSING FABRICS

Don't forget to check the Color Chart (page 21) for a key to the color abbreviations. When choosing your own colors, see Color and Balance (page 12). All the colors in this quilt need to play well together. This technique also makes use of a background color for three of its blocks. Select a color for this role (usually a white or beige).

Kona Colors in this quilt: Avocado, Cosmos, Coral, Pickle, Sage, Sassy Pink, Snow

BUILDING BLOCKS

Let's get a sense of the various "blocks" that this technique includes. When I say "blocks," I am conspicuously miming big air quotes so the world knows these "blocks" are not traditional blocks that quilters use in traditional patterns. These improv "blocks" will not be uniform in size or color. The unifying feature of each "block" (okay, that's the last time I'm using quotes) is the shape. And even that might not be uniform. WAIT! Don't throw this book at the wall yet! Stick with me!

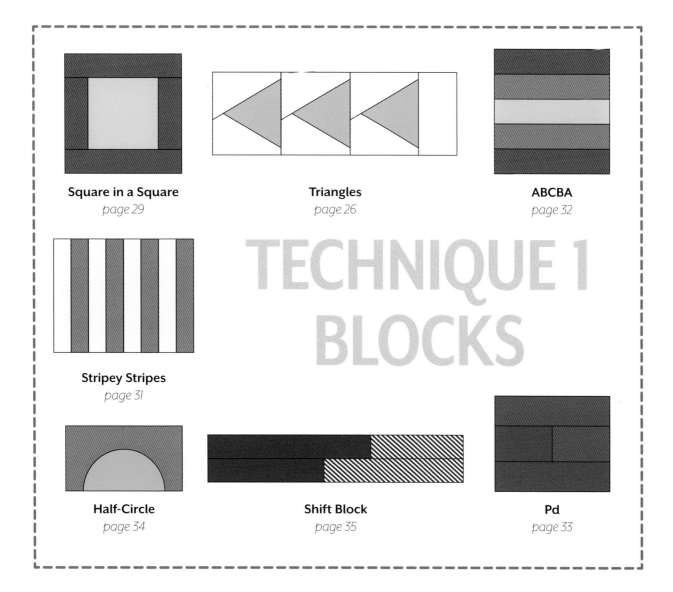

Square in a Square
page 29

Triangles
page 26

ABCBA
page 32

TECHNIQUE 1 BLOCKS

Stripey Stripes
page 31

Half-Circle
page 34

Shift Block
page 35

Pd
page 33

Materials

Yardages are based on 42˝ of usable width.

⅛ yard of 2 colors (A, M)

¼ yard of 2 colors (C, L)

½ yard each of 2 colors (K, S)

½ yard of background color (W)

▶ HOLD UP!

This materials list is just to get you started—enough fabric to practice each block in this technique, but not enough to assemble into one of the projects. It will make 4 Triangles blocks, 2 Square in a Square blocks, 1 Stripey Stripes block, 2 ABCBA blocks, 2 Pd blocks, and 1 Half-Circle block. The sample quilt doesn't contain any Shift blocks, though this chapter also includes instructions to make one, as I often use them in technique 1 quilts. Each project in the book has its own full materials list.

TRIANGLES BLOCK

Choose one color to pair with the background color (S, W).

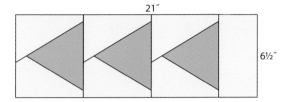

Cutting

You'll need:

Fabric S

- 12 right triangles 4˝ × 7˝
- 6 equilateral 60° triangles, 5¼˝ tall, 6˝ on all sides
- 2 rectangles 7˝ × 3˝

Fabric W

- 12 right triangles 4˝ × 7˝
- 6 equilateral 60° triangles, 5¼˝ tall, 6˝ on all sides
- 2 rectangles 7˝ × 3˝

Equilateral Triangles

1. Stack and align folded yardage of both S and W.

2. Cut a 6˝ × WOF strip from the top. Set aside the rest of the fabric. While still stacked, subcut the strips into 6˝ squares (6 per color). Set aside the extra.

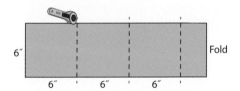

3. Align one stack of squares with the 60° angled line on the cutting mat, so that the line goes through the lower left corner while the sides of the squares are aligned to the horizontal and vertical lines on the mat. Cut one corner off the square, following the line. Repeat with the other stacks. Flip the stacks over horizontally and repeat.

▶ **SAVE THOSE SCRAPS**
I recommend saving the cut-off corners in your scrap basket for later in this book.

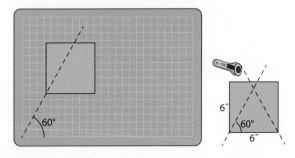

Right Triangles

1. Stack and align folded yardage of both S and W.

▶ **COLOR CHANGE**

If you want some variety, you could use a different color instead of S here. You're the boss!

2. Cut a 7˝ × WOF strip from the top. Set aside the rest of the fabric. While still stacked, subcut the strip into 7˝ × 4˝ rectangles (6 per color). Set aside the extra.

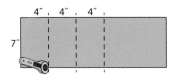

3. Cut diagonally through one stack of rectangles to create 2 right triangles. Repeat for the other stacks. Separate by color.

4. Find the leftover fabric (7˝ wide). Subcut into 2 rectangles 7˝ × 3˝ of each color.

▶ **NOTE**

Kona cotton is the same color on both sides, but not all fabric is. If you're using a fabric with a right and wrong side, when cutting diagonally to create right triangles, cut 2 stacks in one direction, and 2 stacks in the other direction to create mirror-image triangles for the block.

Assembly

1. Right sides together, align a W right triangle (long edge) with an S equilateral triangle. The W triangle should hang ½˝ above the top of the S triangle. Sew together. Make 6 units. Press all seams toward the right triangle.

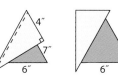

2. Repeat Step 1 to sew the S right triangles to the W equilateral triangles. Make 6 units.

3. Sew the long side of a W right triangle onto the unsewn side of an S equilateral triangle from a Step 1 unit. Use the same alignment from Step 1. Repeat for all 6 units.

4. Repeat Step 3 to attach S right triangles to the 6 Step 2 units with W equilateral triangles.

5. Press seams towards the outside right triangles. Trim all 12 units into 6½˝ × 6½˝ squares.

6. Decide which triangles you want to combine into a block. For now, let's say you want to make blocks of 3 triangles each. Stack 2 units with S equilateral triangles right sides together and facing opposite directions. Pin and sew. Repeat to add a third unit with an S equilateral triangle.

7. Press the seams to one side. Trim to 18½˝ × 6½˝. This is called an S Triangles Block.

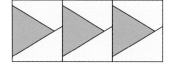

8. Repeat Steps 6–7 to create 4 blocks (2 S blocks, 2 W blocks).

9. Align a W 3″ × 7″ rectangle, right sides together, with the bottom of an S Triangles Block. Pin and sew. Repeat to sew a rectangle to all the Triangles Blocks. The rectangle color should match the right triangle color in the block.

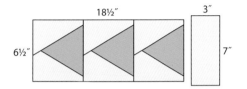

10. Press all seam allowances towards the bottom rectangles. Trim the blocks to 21″ × 6½″.

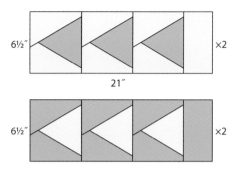

Variations and Use

The most obvious variation to this block is to change the number of triangles in a block. The instructions here suggest 3 in a row. But you could sew just 2 together! Or 4! Six, however, would likely be too many in a row to maintain visual balance across a whole project.

I recommend that you make at least 3 Triangles Blocks for any Technique 1 quilt.

SQUARE IN A SQUARE BLOCK

Choose 2 colors (L, C).

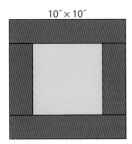

10" × 10"

Cutting

You'll need:

Fabric L:

- 2 squares 6" × 6"

Fabric C:

- 4 rectangles 2½" × 6"
- 4 rectangles 2½" × 10"

1. Cut a 6" × WOF strip from the top of L. Set aside the rest of the fabric. Subcut the strip into 2 squares 6" × 6". Set aside the extra.

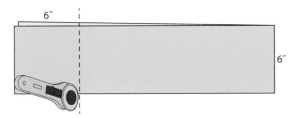

6"

6"

2. Cut a 2½" × WOF strip from the top of C. Repeat to make a second strip. Subcut the strips into 4 rectangles 2½" × 6". Subcut the strips again to make 4 rectangles 2½" × 10".

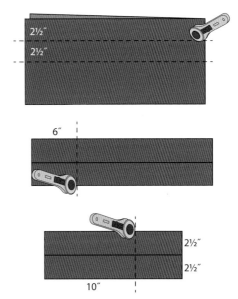

2½"

2½"

6"

2½"

2½"

10"

Assembly

1. Pin and sew 2 C rectangles 2½″ × 6″ to opposite sides of an L square, right sides together. Press the seams toward the C rectangles. Repeat for the second square.

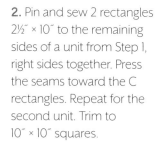

2. Pin and sew 2 rectangles 2½″ × 10″ to the remaining sides of a unit from Step 1, right sides together. Press the seams toward the C rectangles. Repeat for the second unit. Trim to 10″ × 10″ squares.

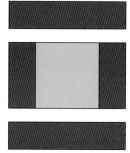

Variations and Use

The variety of this block lies in the sizes of its parts and variety of its colors. Imagine making the inside square bigger or more rectangular. Imagine reversing the inside and outside colors. Some limitations: I don't recommend that the outside strips exceed the width of the internal square. I recommend that you make at least 4 Square in a Square Blocks for any Technique 1 quilt.

STRIPEY STRIPES BLOCK

For this block, pair one color with the background color (W, K).

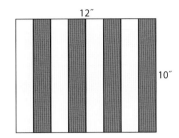

Cutting

You'll need:

Fabric W
- 1 strip 2˝ × WOF

Fabric K
- 1 strip 2˝ × WOF

Refer to Cutting Fabric (page 17) if you need more guidance on cutting the above strips.

Assembly

1. Unfold the strips. Sew the 2 strips, right sides together, lengthwise. Press the seam toward the darker fabric.

2. Mark the center point of the unit from Step 1 and cut in half.

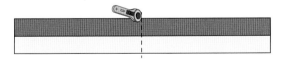

3. Arrange the 2 halves so the stripes alternate colors. Right sides together, pin and sew (W stripe and K stripe should be touching). Press the seam in the same direction as the existing seams. This unit should measure 6½˝ × 21˝.

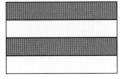

4. Mark the center point of the unit from Step 3 and cut in half.

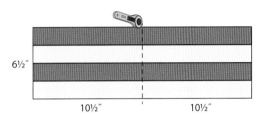

5. Repeat Step 3 with the units from Step 4 to finish the block. Trim to 10˝ × 12˝.

Variations and Use

Your Stripey Stripes might vary in color or length. You could cut your finished Stripey Stripes Block in half again to create 2 separate, super narrow Stripey Stripes Blocks. You could also vary the width of the strips you cut at the start to, say 1¾˝ instead of 2˝. You could even choose two main colors, instead of using a background one! I recommend using at least 3 Stripey Stripes Blocks for any quilt.

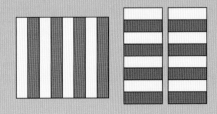

ABCBA BLOCK

Choose 3 colors. I'm using remaining yardage from colors I've already used (L, C, K).

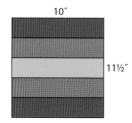

10″

11½″

Cutting

You'll need:

Fabric L

• 1 strip 2½″ × 21″

Fabric C

• 1 strip 2″ × WOF (42″)

Fabric K

• 1 strip 3″ × WOF (42″)

For this block, cut each color separately because the strips vary in width. Refer to Cutting Fabric (page 17) if you need more guidance on cutting the C and K strips.

1. Cut a 2½″ × WOF strip from the top of the L yardage. Subcut the strip in half to make 2 strips 2½″ × 21″. Set aside 1 of the pieces.

▶ PILE OF LONELY PANELS

When you have a strip of excess fabric to set aside while making an ABCBA Block, throw it in a heap that I call the Pile of Lonely Panels. You will use panels from that pile later, when assembling the blocks into bigger blocks.

Assembly

1. Sew the C and K strips, right sides together, lengthwise. Press the seam toward the C fabric.

2. Mark the center of the Step 1 unit and cut in half.

3. Stack the L rectangle, right sides together, with the K strip in 1 unit from Step 2. Pin and sew together. Press the seam toward the K strip.

4. Sew the 2 units from Step 2 and Step 3 together, joining the K and L strips. Press the seam toward the K strip.

5. Cut the unit from Step 4 in half vertically to make 2 ABCBA Blocks. Trim to 10″ × 10″ each.

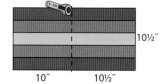

10½″

10″   10½″

Variations and Use

The most obvious variation to make on this block is to vary the widths of the fabric strips. You can also cut the unit from Step 4 into narrower individual blocks. Just be sure to maintain the order of the colors, which should mirror around the center color— just like the letters ABCBA. I recommend using at least four ABCBA Blocks for any quilt.

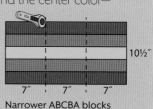

10½″

7″   7″   7″

Narrower ABCBA blocks

PD BLOCK

This block is called the
Pd block because visually, it
looks like 2 blocks fitted
together like a letter P and
letter d. Get it? Choose
2 colors (A,M).

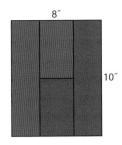

8″

10″

Cutting

You'll need:

Fabric A

- 2 rectangles 3″ × 5½″
- 3 rectangles 3″ × 10½″

Fabric M

- 2 rectangles 3″ × 5½″
- 3 rectangles 3″ × 10½″

1. Stack and align folded A and M yardage. Cut a
3″ × WOF strip. Unfold the strips, and cut them in
half. Stack them again.

2. Cut the strips in half again, resulting in
8 rectangles 3″ × 10½″ (4 of each color).

3. Stack 1 rectangle 3″ × 10½″ of each color. Cut in
half again, resulting in 4 rectangles 3″ × 5⅓″ (2 of each
color).

Assembly

1. Right sides together, pin and sew
2 rectangles 3″ × 5¼″, 1 of each
color, together on 1 of the short sides. Press the
seam towards the darker color.

2. Right sides together, pin and sew
the unit from Step 1 with a 3″ × 10½″
A rectangle along 1 long side. Press
the seam towards the A rectangle.

3. Repeat Step 2 to attach
1 M rectangle 3″ × 10½″ to the unit
from Step 2. Press the seam
towards the M rectangle. Trim to
a 10″ × 8″ rectangle.

5. Repeat Steps 1–3 to make a second block. Set
aside all leftover scraps.

Variations and Use

You might vary the widths of the
panels. You might also vary where you
place the break in the middle panel.
You might rotate or flip the block! Go
nuts! I recommend using at least 4 Pd
Blocks in any quilt.

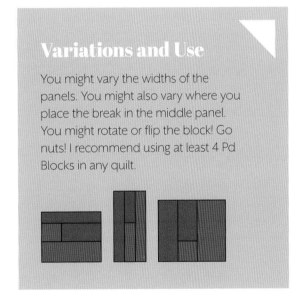

HALF-CIRCLE BLOCK

Deep breaths here, people. Listen, I'm gonna make this easy, but if you'd rather not do curves right now, don't! Seriously, This technique looks just as fabulous without any curved pieces. Choose 2 colors (K, S).

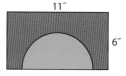

11″

6″

Cutting

See Templates (page 11).

Color K

· 1 half-circle arch from Half-Circle Outside Template

Color S

· 1 half-circle from Half-Circle Inside Template

Assembly

I hate using pins. They are fiddly and hard to sew around and pokey for goodness' sake. But alas, for half-circles, you probably should grab the pins.

1. Fold both cut pieces in half and crease the middles with your finger.

2. Open both pieces up. Orient the K piece so that the cut out portion faces away from you. Place the S piece on top with the flat edge

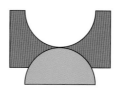

nearest to you, right sides together. Align the center creases of both pieces. Pin.

3. Flip the unit over, keeping the pin in place. Scoot, stretch, and scrunch the K piece around the S piece, pinning as you go so that the edges are lined up.

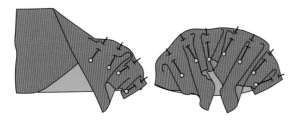

❚ DON'T SKIP THIS TIP! ❚

Keeping the needle in the down position as you take pins out will help keep the fabric from sliding.

4. Sew around the top of the half-circle, removing pins as you go. Unfold and press the seam toward the darker fabric. Trim the block to be a 6″ × 11″ rectangle.

Variations and Use

I often add a narrow bottom panel to the Half-Circle Block. Use the same color as the exterior half-circle piece

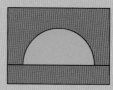

(color K in this case.) Cut a 2½″ × 11 K strip and sew to the bottom of the finished block. I recommend using at least 2 Half-Circle Blocks for any quilt.

Try making the half-circle out of 2 different colors.

You might even sew triangles together to make the half-circle. You can use the triangles you cut off when making the Triangles Block (page 26). See Half-Circle Block Variation: Whirligigs (page 99) for assembly instructions.

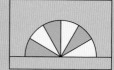

SHIFT BLOCK

This block is helpful to use as a gap-filler. Practice with 2 colors (A, M). These 2 colors should have enough leftover yardage to make the block. The illustrations pictured here show the Shift block in the colors used in The (Not-Boring) Neutral Quilt (page 96).

22″

4½″

Cutting

You'll need:

Fabric A

· 2 rectangles 2½″ × 14″

Fabric M

· 2 rectangles 2½″ × 14″

1. Stack and align folded A and M yardage. Cut a 2½″ × WOF strip from the top.

2. Unfold the strips and cut a 2½″ × 14″ rectangle from each color. Set aside the remaining fabric.

Assembly

1. Right sides together, sew 1 rectangle of each color together along 1 short side. Repeat for the remaining 2 rectangles. Press seams toward the A rectangles.

2. Align the units from Step 1 so their seams are even. Then, shift the top unit to the right as far as you desire. Right sides together, pin and sew the shifted units together.

3. Press the seam to one side. Trim the excess fabric, making a 4½″ × 22″ block.

ASSEMBLING ALL THE BLOCKS

If you could see me now, you'd see me wiggling my fingers like a kid about to dig into a bag of gummy bears. This is literally my favorite part of the whole thing. The joy of creating! The thrill of assembling the puzzle!

If you've been following the instructions as is, you've made a total of 12 blocks. Those were perfect for practicing Technique 1 Blocks, but, if you want to assemble them into a project, you'll need more blocks. So go sew as your heart desires, or, you can follow along with the assembly technique here, and then check out A Quilt To Impress Your Mother-In-Law (page 82) or The (Not-Boring) Neutral Quilt (page 96) for more direction on how many and which kinds of blocks to make for a full-sized project.

CREATING DOUBLE AND TRIPLE BLOCKS

As we start to think about how to assemble a whole project, we start small. The first step is to sew the single blocks into pairs (or trios). We call those pairs *Double Blocks* (or *Triple Blocks*).

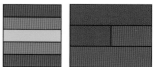

Look for 2 blocks that are similar in size. Maybe you found an ABCBA block (10˝ × 11½˝) and a Pd Block (10˝ × 8˝). Both of these blocks have sides that are 10˝! Yes! Sewing those 10˝ sides together (right sides facing each other, always) would make for a Double Block that was about 10˝ × 19.˝

After you combine the blocks that match well, you will find that there are some blocks that don't match up. So, you will need to add panels and/or trim blocks to make blocks fit together. (You can do this!)

Several double or triple blocks I created for the Technique 1 sample quilt.

Adding Panels

Example 1 (below) shows when adding a panel is useful. The Stripey Stripes Block is too short to match with the Triangles Block. So, add an 8″ × 9″ rectangle panel onto the side of the Stripey Stripes Block to make it longer. I chose color M for the panel. This is when your Pile of Lonely Panels really comes in handy.

You don't need to do the math to figure out the dimensions of the M rectangle. Just use the ruler to measure the approximate length of the gap the M panel will fill and round up, making the panel larger than it needs to be. The short sides of the rectangle should be the same as the Stripey Stripes block, 10.″ Sew the panel and Stripey Stripes Blocks together. Press the seam to the side. Sew the new unit to the Triangles Block. Trim off any extra fabric.

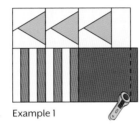

Example 1

Don't be afraid to add a *two-color* large panel if needed. In Example 2, adding one giant 4″ × 20″ one-color panel of fabric underneath the Triangle Block would be an attention hog, so instead I sewed together 2 rectangles 4″ × 11″ first (K & L). Then I sewed the KL panel to the Triangles Block. Then, since they now have a matching dimension, I sewed both of those to a Pd Block.

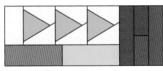

Example 2

Trimming Blocks

If a block is slightly too big, you can also trim it to fit with a smaller block. To pair a 10″ × 11½″ ABCBA Block with a 6″ × 11″ Half-Circle Block, the Half-Circle Block would be just ½″ too short. We could add a small panel to the Half-Circle block, but that tiny panel would stand out as too small. So, instead trim the ABCBA Block by

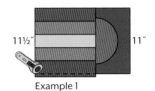

Example 1

½.″ Note that there are some places where blocks shouldn't be cut—doing so leaves weird shapes and remnants. For Half-Circle blocks, try to only cut vertically through the center of the circle, or to cut an equal amount from each short side of the rectangular part of the block without cutting the circle. For Triangle Blocks, cut off whole shapes, not partial shapes. For the Square in a Square Block, make sure none of the outside panels are cut narrower than 2.″

In Example 2, the Square in a Square Block is too short for the Triangles block. Cutting the Triangles Block to match with the width of the Square in a Square Block would cut off part of one of the triangles. Thumbs down. So instead of trimming there, add a 2½″ wide panel to the Square in a Square, extending it, and allowing you to cleanly trim the third triangle off.

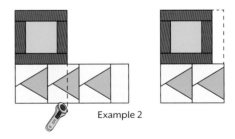

Example 2

⫻ LEAVE SOME UNCOUPLED ⫻

It is a good idea to leave some of the blocks as single blocks. As you combine Double Blocks together in the next section, you might need a few single blocks to fill space.

DOUBLE AND TRIPLE BLOCK EXAMPLES

BUILDING BIG BLOCKS

In the previous step, you sewed single blocks into Double or Triple Blocks based on their sizes. Now we want to start sewing those into even bigger blocks which we will call (you guessed it): Big Blocks.

Making a Big Block is as simple as sewing 2 Double/Triple Blocks together in a way that makes sense. I start by looking for 2 Double Blocks that look similar in size. I rotate them around until I find 2 sides that can be sewn together in an appealing way. Since they probably aren't exactly the same size, I either add a panel to the shorter Double Block or trim a portion off of the longer Double Block. Then, I sew them together and press the seam toward one side (whichever side seems less bulky.)

As you combine blocks, don't forget about color! Remember, you don't want a pool of color or shape all in one corner of the quilt top and nowhere else. So in each of these Big Blocks, try to have a variety of colors and shapes. You'll get the hang of it once you start. And if you need to take blocks apart later, the Earth will keep spinning around the sun, I promise. Give yourself space to arrange, rearrange, spin, rotate and move the Double Blocks all around.

An example of several Big Blocks blocks created for the Technique 1 sample quilt.

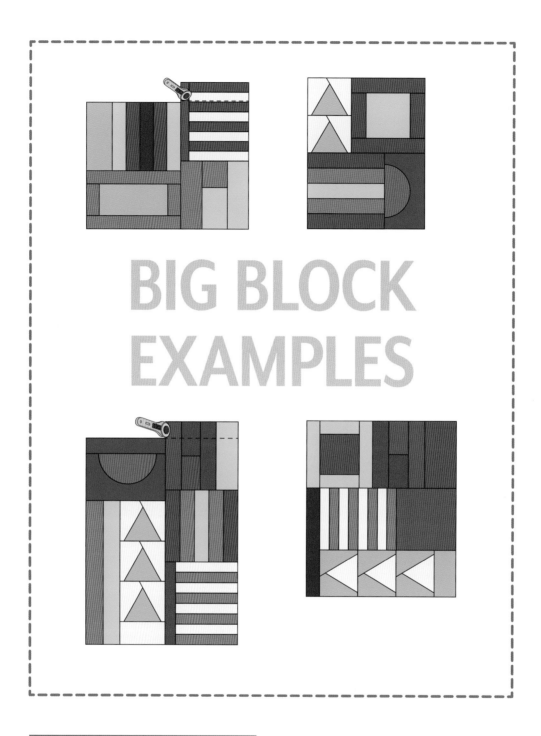

PRESSING AND TRIMMING

Press the seams in the Big Blocks flat using a hot iron. Press down, making sure you don't distort the shapes. Periodically trim the sides of the Big Blocks as you piece, to make the edges crisp and the angles 90 degrees. The Big Blocks do not need to be uniform in size and they do not have to be squares, though some might be. They all should be some type of rectangle with 90° corners.

PUZZLING IT OUT

Combining Big Blocks into a quilt top takes some puzzling over.

1. Lay all of the Big Blocks out on the floor.

2. Find 2 Big Blocks that are similar in size, remembering that they won't be exactly the same.

3. Make 2 sides of those Big Blocks the same length by:

- Trimming off a portion of the longer Big Block
- Adding panels to the shorter Big Block
- Adding another single or double block to the shorter Big Block

4. Pin those 2 same-length sides and sew. Press the seam and double check the corners are still 90°, trimming if needed.

Joining Big Blocks Together

Example 1 shows how 2 Big Blocks might fit together. There are a few reasons I think that these are good fits. I like that the Triangles Blocks are pointing in different directions. I like that the Stripey Stripes are, too. I like that there aren't any of the same colors from both big blocks touching each other on the connecting side. To make things fit better, I can trim off the top edge of Big Block 1, and I can add something to the bottom of Big Block 2.

In the second example, I don't like that separate color K pieces would touch where the 2 big blocks are being joined. So, I'm adding 2 panels of fabric between the 2 big blocks instead of connecting them directly. Then, after assembly I can trim off the side from Big Block 3, and the bottom from Big Block 4. Easy peasy, lemon squeezy.

Big Block 1   Big Block 2

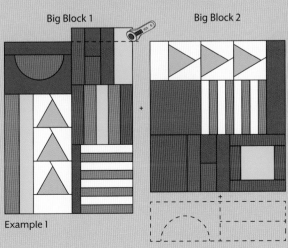

Example 1

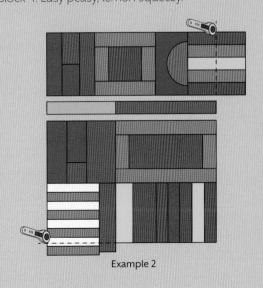

Example 2

5. Now, place this huge, two-Big-Block unit back on the floor. Lay out the other Big Blocks around it. Arrange and rearrange the other Big Blocks, planning how all the rest could fit in, too. Periodically do The Spiderweb Check (page 15) to ensure things are balanced.

As you arrange the rest of the Big Blocks together, you might realize you still have empty spaces in the puzzle. Or, maybe what you have left doesn't have the colors or shapes you need. The solution: make more puzzle pieces (blocks)! Analyze the sizes of the empty spaces you have and determine whether you need a single block, double block, or even another Big Block. Then go back and make those to fit the empty spaces.

▶ DISASSEMBLY

You might find that only part of a Big Block fits in the space you need. Don't get too precious about cutting apart blocks—you can always save the cut-off for another project another day. If you feel reluctant to cut a block, fold it over first to see how it would look.

Evaluate the Layout

Once you have all of the Big Blocks (and any other blocks and panels you added to make the puzzle fit) arranged in a way that seems to work—evaluate the layout for balance. Step back and ask yourself some questions, like a *Choose Your Own Adventure!*

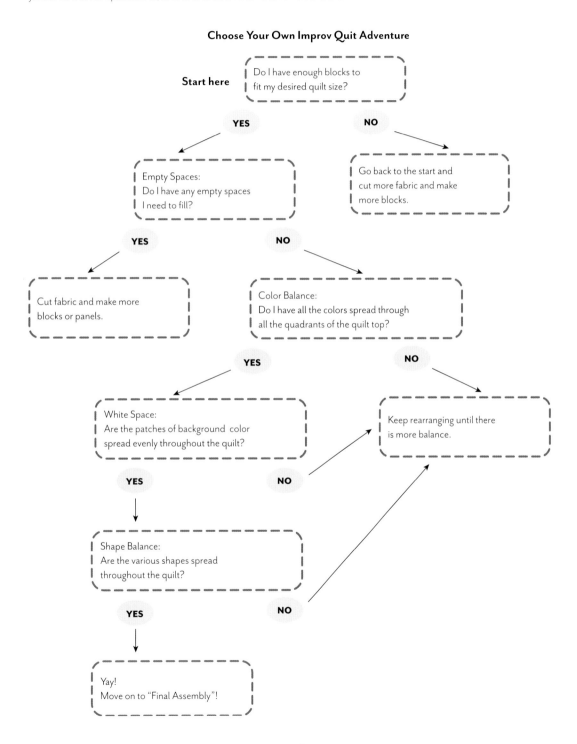

Choose Your Own Improv Quit Adventure

Start here → Do I have enough blocks to fit my desired quilt size?

YES → Empty Spaces: Do I have any empty spaces I need to fill?

NO → Go back to the start and cut more fabric and make more blocks.

Empty Spaces **YES** → Cut fabric and make more blocks or panels.

Empty Spaces **NO** → Color Balance: Do I have all the colors spread through all the quadrants of the quilt top?

Color Balance **YES** → White Space: Are the patches of background color spread evenly throughout the quilt?

Color Balance **NO** → Keep rearranging until there is more balance.

White Space **YES** → Shape Balance: Are the various shapes spread throughout the quilt?

White Space **NO** → Keep rearranging until there is more balance.

Shape Balance **YES** → Yay! Move on to "Final Assembly"!

Shape Balance **NO** → Keep rearranging until there is more balance.

FINAL ASSEMBLY: SEWING IT ALL TOGETHER

Before you start sewing the big blocks and extra pieces together, take a photo of it all. It's nice to refer back to it if you forget which piece goes where. Then, sew it all together into a quilt top. Start with the smallest pieces. Press seams as you go, avoiding bulk. Make sure corners are 90° and edges are trimmed crisp. Before you know it, you'll have every piece of the puzzle in place.

▶ REMEMBER

You can *always* add more blocks! The beautiful thing about improv quilting is that the quilt top is never finished until you feel done with it. If you assemble a quilt top here and realize it is smaller than you had hoped, go make more blocks and add them to the top, bottom, or sides.

Assembly Summary

1. Single Block Stage: Make individual blocks

2. Double Block Stage: Combine single blocks into double or triple blocks*

3. Big Block Stage: Combine double and triple blocks into Big Blocks *

4. Puzzling Stage: Sew Big Blocks together, checking for balance, and add panels, single, double, or triple blocks as necessary to make the quilt flimsy*

Combine blocks by sewing together on 2 sides of similar size, adding panels or trimming as needed

Example layout from some of the example big blocks

Okay fine, the sample quilt top has already been sandwiched and quilted in this photo!

IMPROV TECHNIQUE 2
Sparse and Geometric Improv

Technique 2 sample quilt layout illustration

FINAL DIMENSIONS: 87˝ × 70˝

The two other improvisational techniques in this book work with fabric pieces that are relatively small. This technique, however, works with fabric pieces that are much larger. Working with larger pieces usually means quicker piecing—it's perfect for making large quilts in a short amount of time and with a lot of creative freedom.

This technique is used to make the Duochrome Bed Quilt (page 102) and the Get Going Duffle (page 120).

CHOOSING FABRICS

The Kona colors used in the sample quilt are the same as used in all illustrations: Amber, Blueprint, Cactus, Cantaloupe, Cosmos, Gotham Gray, Pansy, Pistachio, Teal.

 Don't forget to check the Color Chart (page 21) for a key to the color abbreviations. When choosing your own colors, see Color and Balance (page 12). This quilt is great for using just 2 colors, but in this sample, I featured 12 colors. Any middle ground between these two options works too. Your background color needs to be consistent, but it does not need to white or beige!

 Also, I recommend avoiding patterned fabrics altogether for this technique to avoid imbalance and busyness.

4 color quilt

BLOCK LAYOUTS: COLUMNS ARE KEY

All Technique 2 quilts are laid out into columns. Each column contains a few 24″ × 24″ squares and 1 rectangle 18″ × 24″. The number of columns in a quilt depends on desired quilt size.

47½″ / 65″

24″ × 24″	24″ × 24″
24″ × 24″	24″ × 24″
18″ × 24″	18″ × 24″

Throw Quilt size: 47½″ × 65″
Layout: 2 columns

71″ / 88½″

24″ × 24″	24″ × 24″	24″ × 24″
24″ × 24″	24″ × 24″	24″ × 24″
24″ × 24″	24″ × 24″	24″ × 24″
18″ × 24″	18″ × 24″	18″ × 24″

Twin Quilt size: 71″ × 88½″
Layout: 3 columns

106″ / 88½″

24″ × 24″	24″ × 24″	24″ × 12″	24″ × 24″	24″ × 24″
24″ × 24″	24″ × 24″	24″ × 12″	24″ × 24″	24″ × 24″
24″ × 24″	24″ × 24″	24″ × 12″	24″ × 24″	24″ × 24″
18″ × 24″	18″ × 24″	18″ × 12″	18″ × 24″	18″ × 24″

Full/Queen Quilt size: 88½″ × 106″
Layout: 4½ columns

106″ / 112″

24″ × 24″	24″ × 24″	24″ × 12″	24″ × 24″	24″ × 24″
24″ × 24″	24″ × 24″	24″ × 12″	24″ × 24″	24″ × 24″
24″ × 24″	24″ × 24″	24″ × 12″	24″ × 24″	24″ × 24″
24″ × 24″	24″ × 24″	24″ × 12″	24″ × 24″	24″ × 24″
18″ × 24″	18″ × 24″	18″ × 12″	18″ × 24″	18″ × 24″

Giant Quilt size: 106″ × 112″
Layout: 4½ columns

THE BOSS MAKES THE CHOICES

There are several decisions to make when planning a Technique 2 improv design. Good news! YOU are the boss, so YOU get to decide!

Location of Rectangle Block

Each column contains 1 rectangle block 18˝ × 24˝ (to go with the other square blocks.) In the illustrations on the previous page, it is shown at the bottom of each column. But the rectangle can really be located anywhere within the column.

Block Design

The actual design of each block is also up to you. This chapter provides step-by-step directions of several of my block designs, but if you want to design your own or use other 24˝ blocks, do it boss!

Block Orientation

Because (most of) the blocks are square and solid fabric isn't directional, there are 4 different ways to orient each block. Just rotating 90° gives a block an entirely different look. Note that the rectangle block in each column must remain horizontal, so it can only be rotated by 180°.

Location of Half Column

The 2 largest quilt sizes each contain a half column. The half column is only 12˝ wide so the blocks are called *halfsies*. Where that half column falls in the overall layout is totally up to you!

BUILDING BLOCKS

Like I mentioned, the possibilities are endless when choosing blocks to fit into this technique—any blocks that fit into the Block Layouts (page 48) will work. As you complete the projects in the back half of the book, you'll want to refer back to these cutting and assembly instructions frequently.

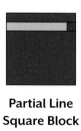

Partial Line Square Block
page 52

Double Line Square Block
page 53

Little Corner Square Block
page 53

Big Bubba Square Block
page 54

Slope Square Block
page 54

SQUARE BLOCKS

Half Square Triangle (HST) Square Block
page 55

Equilateral Triangle (ET) Square Block
page 55

Quarter Round Square Block
page 56

Empty Square Block
page 57

RECTANGLE BLOCKS

**Round
Rectangle Block**
page 57

**Power Rectangle
Block**
page 58

**One Strip
Rectangle Block**
page 58

HALFSIE BLOCKS
for half-columns

**Almost Full Halfsie
Rectangle**
page 59

**Almost Full
Halfsie Square**
page 59

▶ HOLD UP!

The material list here is just to get you started on each of the blocks—enough fabric to practice each block in this technique, but not enough to assemble into a project. Each set of instructions will make one block, unless otherwise noted in the block instructions. Each project in the book has its own full materials list.

◀ SAVE THOSE CUT-OFFS ▶

As you practice making the blocks, save the scraps of fabric yardage you cut off. You'll need them as you progress through making the blocks and your yardage starts shrinking.

PARTIAL LINE SQUARE BLOCK

Choose one color and the background color (O, GG).

Cutting

You'll need:

Fabric O

· 1 strip 3½˝ × 21˝

Fabric GG

· 1 square 3½˝ × 3½˝

· 1 rectangle 3½˝ × 24˝

· 1 rectangle 18˝ × 24˝

1. Stack and align GG and O yardage. Cut a strip 3½˝ × WOF (one of each color). Set aside the O yardage.

2. From the remaining GG yardage, cut a rectangle 18˝ × WOF.

3. Cut the 18˝ strip of GG fabric into a rectangle 18˝ × 24˝. Set aside the rest of the piece. Cut the 3½˝ GG strip into a 3½˝ × 24˝ strip. From the remaining 3½˝ strip, cut a 3½˝ × 3½˝ square. Set aside the rest of the piece.

4. Cut the O strip into a 3½˝ × 21˝ rectangle. Set aside the rest of the strip.

Assembly

1. Pin and sew the GG square to the O strip, right sides together. Press the seam in one direction.

2. Pin and sew the unit from Step 1 to the 3½˝ × 24˝ rectangle along one long edge. Press the seam toward the GG fabric.

3. Pin and sew the unit from Step 2 to the remaining rectangle. The long O edge and the long GG edge should attach. Press the seam towards the GG fabric. Trim to a 24˝ × 24˝ square.

DOUBLE LINE SQUARE BLOCK

Choose one color and the background color (E, GG).

Cutting

You'll need:

Color GG
- 1 rectangle 9″ × 24″
- 1 rectangle 6½″ × 24″

Color E
- 1 rectangle 6½″ × 24″
- 1 strip 3½″ × 24″

1. From the GG yardage, cut a strip 9″ × WOF and a strip 6½″ × WOF. Set aside the rest of the yardage.

2. Cut the 9″ strip into a 9″ × 24″ rectangle. Cut the 6½″ strip into a 6½″ × 24″ rectangle.

3. Repeat Steps 1–2 with the E yardage, cutting a 3½″ × WOF strip instead of a 9″ × WOF strip.

Assembly

1. Line up the rectangles horizontally as shown. Pin and sew each GG rectangle to the E rectangle below it, creating 2 units. Press the seams to one side.

2. Pin and sew the 2 units from Step 1 together, attaching the 6½″ × 24″ E and GG rectangles. Press the seam toward E. Trim to a 24″ × 24″ square.

LITTLE CORNER SQUARE BLOCK

Choose one color and the background color (E, GG).

Cutting

You'll need:

Fabric GG
- 1 rectangle 9″ × 6½″
- 1 rectangle 15½″ × 24″

Fabric E
- 1 rectangle 9″ × 18″

1. Find a scrap of GG fabric 9″ × 16″ (set aside from the Double Line Square Block). Cut into a 9″ × 6½″ rectangle. Cut from yardage if needed.

2. From the GG yardage, cut a strip 24″ × WOF. Set aside the rest of the yardage. Subcut the strip into a rectangle 15½″ × 24″.

3. From the E yardage, cut a 9″ × WOF strip. Set aside the rest of the E yardage. Subcut the strip into a 9″ × 18″ rectangle.

Assembly

1. Pin and sew the 9″ sides of the GG rectangle and E rectangle. Press the seam to one side.

2. Pin and sew the unit from Step 1 to the remaining GG rectangle. Press the seam toward the GG fabric. Trim to a 24″ × 24″ square.

BIG BUBBA SQUARE BLOCK

Choose one color (maybe your favorite!) and the background color (R, GG).

Cutting

You'll need:

Fabric GG

- 1 rectangle 3½˝ × 24˝
- 1 rectangle 6½˝ × 21˝

Fabric R

- 1 rectangle 18˝ × 21˝

1. Cut two GG rectangles, one 3½˝ × 24˝ and one 6½˝ × 21˝. You should be able to cut these from the GG scraps you made when cutting the shapes for the previous blocks instead of cutting from the GG yardage.

2. From the R yardage, cut a strip 18˝ × WOF. Trim into a rectangle 18˝ × 21˝.

Assembly

1. Pin and sew the 21˝ sides of the 6½˝ GG rectangle and the R rectangle. Press the seam toward the GG fabric.

2. Pin and sew the Step 1 unit to the remaining GG rectangle on the 24˝ sides. Press the seam toward the GG fabric. Trim to a 24˝ × 24˝ square.

SLOPE SQUARE BLOCK

These instructions will make 2 identical Slope Square Blocks. Choose one color and the background color (O, GG).

Cutting

You'll need:

Fabric GG

- 2 rectangles 9½˝ × 24˝
- 1 rectangle 16˝ × 25˝:

Subcut into 2 right triangles

Fabric O

- 1 rectangle 16˝ × 25˝:

Subcut into 2 right triangles

1. From the GG yardage, cut a 25˝ × WOF strip. Set aside the rest of the yardage. Subcut 2 rectangles 9½˝ × 25˝ from the strip. Unfold the remaining strip and subcut into a rectangle 16˝ × 25˝.

2. From the O yardage, cut a 16˝ × WOF strip. Subcut into a rectangle 16˝ × 25˝.

3. Stack the 2 rectangles 16˝ × 25˝. Cut diagonally, corner to corner, resulting in 4 triangles.

Assembly

1. Pin and sew a GG triangle to an O triangle along the hypotenuse. Repeat with the other pair of triangles. Press the seams toward O.

2. Pin and sew a 9½˝ × 24˝ rectangle to a unit from Step 1 at the 24˝ sides. Repeat with the second rectangle and unit. Press the seams toward the GG rectangle. Trim into a 24˝ × 24˝ square. This block often requires extra trimming.

HALF-SQUARE TRIANGLE (HST) SQUARE BLOCK

These instructions will make 2 identical HST Square Blocks. Choose one color and the background color (C, GG).

Cutting

You'll need:

Fabric GG

- 25˝ × 25˝ square:

Subcut into 2 right triangles

Fabric C

- 25˝ × 25˝ square:

Subcut into 2 right triangles

1. From the GG yardage, cut a strip 25˝ × WOF. Unfold, and subcut into a 25˝ × 25˝ square. Set aside the rest of the yardage.

2. Repeat Step 1 with the C yardage.

3. Stack the 2 squares. Cut diagonally, corner to corner, resulting in 4 triangles.

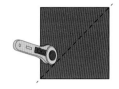

Assembly

1. Pin and sew a C triangle to a GG triangle along the hypotenuse. Press the seam to one side. Repeat with the other 2 triangles. Trim to a 24˝ × 24˝ square.

EQUILATERAL TRIANGLE (ET) SQUARE BLOCK

Choose one color and the background color (H, GG).

Cutting

You'll need:

Fabric GG

- 1 strip 3½˝ × 24˝
- 1 rectangle 15˝ × 26˝:

Subcut into 2 right triangles

Fabric H

- 1 equilateral triangle, 20⅔˝ tall and 24˝ on all sides

1. Cut a GG rectangle 10˝ × 24˝ (use the scraps you cut from the previous blocks before cutting into your GG yardage). Subcut into a strip 3½˝ × 24˝.

2. From the GG yardage, cut a strip 15˝ × WOF. Subcut into a rectangle 15˝ × 26˝. Subcut again, this time diagonally from corner to corner, to make 2 right triangles.

3. From the H yardage, cut a strip 24˝ × WOF. Subcut into a 24˝ × 24˝ square.

4. Align the square with the 60° angled line on the cutting mat. Cut one corner off the square, following the line. Flip the square over horizontally and repeat.

Assembly

1. Right sides together, align a GG right triangle (long edge) with the H equilateral triangle. The GG triangle should hang ½″ above the top of the H triangle. Pin and sew together. Press the seam toward the GG triangle.

2. Repeat Step 1 to sew the second GG triangle to the other side of the H triangle.

3. Trim the extra tails and corners from the block. Trim the block to be 24″ wide, cutting an equal amount of fabric from each edge.

4. Pin and sew the remaining GG rectangle to the top of the unit from Step 3. Press the seam toward the GG rectangle. Trim to a 24″ × 24″ square, removing from the top, bottom, or both to reduce the height.

QUARTER ROUND SQUARE BLOCK

Choose one color and the background color (BB, GG). See Templates (page 11).

Cutting

Fabric GG

· 1 rectangle 22″ × 25″ skating ramp from Quarter Round Square Outside Template

· 1 rectangle 3½″ × 25″

Fabric BB

· 1 quarter circle from Quarter Round Square Inside Template

▶ **TEMPLATES BY HAND, BABY!**

If you don't want to print out the template, you can do it by hand. Tie a length of string to the end of a pencil. Measure 22″ from the pencil tip to the end of the string. Hold the end of the string in the bottom right corner of a 22″ × 22″ square of paper. Slowly move the pencil toward the top left corner of the paper square, maintaining tension on the string.

1. From the GG yardage, cut 1 rectangle 25″ × WOF. Subcut into 1 rectangle 25″ × 3½″ and 1 rectangle 22″ × 25″. Use the Quarter Round Square Outside Template to cut the skating ramp from the 22″ × 25″ rectangle.

2. Use the Quarter Round Square Inside Template to cut the quarter circle from the BB yardage.

Assembly

1. Fold both cut pieces in half and crease the middles with your finger.

2. Open both pieces up. Orient the GG skating ramp so that the cut out portion faces away from you. Place the BB piece on top with the rounded edge facing away from you, right sides together. Align the center creases of both pieces. Pin.

3. Flip the unit over. Scoot, scrunch, and stretch the GG piece around the BB piece, pinning as you go so that the edges are lined up.

4. Sew around the top of the half-circle, removing pins as you go. Unfold and press the seam toward GG. Square the corners.

5. Pin and sew the unit from Step 4 to the remaining rectangle as shown. Press the seam towards GG. Trim to a 24″ × 24″ square.

EMPTY SQUARE BLOCK

The Empty Square Block might seem like the saddest block ever. But can be, in fact, one of the most important blocks in improv Technique 2. Having a whole block of negative space is a powerful tool. Cut a 24˝ × 24˝ square from one color (GG). You can just as easily make this an 18˝ × 24˝ rectangle if you want to!

CREATING RECTANGLE BLOCKS

Remember that Technique 2 Rectangle Blocks are 18˝ × 24.˝

ROUND RECTANGLE BLOCK

Choose one color and the background color (II, GG). See Templates (page 11).

Cutting

You'll need:

Fabric GG

- 24½˝ × 19˝ rectangle skating ramp using the Round Rectangle Outside Template

Fabric II

- 1 semi circle using the Round Rectangle Inside Template

▶ **BY HAND, AGAIN!**

If you want to make your own templates, follow the instructions in Templates By Hand, Baby! (page 56). Measure 18½˝ instead of 22.˝

1. From the GG yardage, cut a 19˝ × WOF strip. Subcut into a rectangle 19˝ × 24½.˝ Use the Round Rectangle Outside Template to cut the skating ramp.

2. Cut the semi circle from the II yardage using the Round Rectangle Inside Template.

Assembly

To assemble this block, follow the instructions in Quarter Round Square Block: Assembly (page 56). Trim to an 18˝ × 24˝ rectangle.

POWER RECTANGLE BLOCK

Choose one color and the background color (M, GG).

Cutting

You'll need:

Fabric GG

• 1 rectangle 6½″ × 18″

Fabric M

• 1 square 18″ × 18″

1. Cut a GG rectangle 6½″ × 18″ (use the scraps left over from cutting other blocks before cutting into yardage again).

2. From the M yardage, cut an 18″ × 18″ square.

Assembly

1. Pin and sew the square and rectangle together along 18″ sides. Press the seam toward GG. Trim to 18″ × 24″.

ONE STRIP RECTANGLE BLOCK

Choose one color and the background color (P, GG).

Cutting

You'll need:

Fabric GG

• 1 strip 3½″ × 24″

• 1 rectangle 12″ × 24″

Fabric P

• 1 strip 3½″ × 24″

1. From GG, cut 1 strip 3½″ × 24″ and 1 rectangle 12″ × 24″. Again, use GG scraps for this.

2. Find a P scrap and trim to 3½″ × 24″.

Assembly

1. Pin and sew the 2 rectangles 3½″ × 24″ along one long side. Press the seam toward GG.

2. Pin and sew the unit from Step 1 to the 12″ × 24″ rectangle along the 24″ side, matching the GG and P edges. Press the seam toward GG. Trim to an 18″ × 24″ rectangle.

CREATING HALFSIE BLOCKS

If you look back at Block Layouts (page 48), you'll see that the larger sizes have a half-width column. This column is made up of 12″ × 24″ and 12″ × 18″ rectangles, which I call *halfsies*.

Make halfsie blocks (see below), or chop the square blocks in half; Big Bubba Square Blocks (page 54) and Empty Square Blocks (page 57) are the best candidates.

ALMOST FULL HALFSIE RECTANGLE

Choose one color and the background color (E, GG).

Cutting

You'll need:

Fabric GG

· 1 strip 18″ × 3½″

Fabric E

· 1 rectangle 18″ × 9″

1. Cut a GG scrap to make a rectangle 18″ × 3½″.

2. Find an E scrap 9″ × 21″ (from the Little Corner Square Block). Cut to a rectangle 18″ × 9″.

Assembly

1. Pin and sew the 2 rectangles along the 18″ sides. Press the seam toward GG. Trim to 18″ × 12″.

ALMOST FULL HALFSIE SQUARE

Choose one color and the background color (M, GG).

Cutting

You'll need:

Fabric GG

· 1 rectangle 18″ × 3½″

· 1 rectangle 6½″ × 12″

Fabric M

· 1 rectangle 18″ × 9″

1. Use GG scraps to cut 1 rectangle 18″ × 3½″ and 1 rectangle 6½″ × 12″.

2. Find an M scrap 9″ × 21″ (from the Power Rectangle Block). Cut into an 18″ × 9″ rectangle.

Assembly

1. Pin and sew the 2 rectangles with 18″ sides. Press the seam toward GG.

2. Pin and sew the unit from Step 1 to the remaining rectangle, aligning the 6½″ sides. Press the seam toward GG. Trim to 12″ × 24″.

ASSEMBLING ALL THE BLOCKS

This is the best part. The blocks are created, pressed, trimmed and sparkling. Now you get to arrange, rearrange, rotate, spin, and repeat. If you've been following the instructions as is, you've made 11 square blocks and 3 rectangle blocks. (You may have also made an Empty Rectangle Block, but I am not counting that in the total here.) You now have enough blocks to make a Technique 2 twin size quilt!

LAYING IT ALL OUT

Refer back to Block Layouts (page 48) as much as needed. Lay the blocks out on the floor in the column format for the Twin. Here are a few tips for arranging and rearranging:

1. Move the rectangle around within its column. Remember the rectangle can be placed anywhere in the column.

2. Play with negative space. Try replacing a shape block with an empty block and see how the balance changes.

3. Rotate the blocks by 90°. Just turning the blocks on their sides can give an entirely different feel to the quilt. Make sure similar shapes are rotated in different ways.

4. Spread out similar shapes. If you are working with 2 curved blocks, for example, don't put them immediately next to each other.

5. Balance the weight of shapes. You'll notice that some blocks are "light" and have just a small section of color. Some blocks, on the other hand, are "heavy" with mostly color. Intermix them.

6. Be judicious about which shapes touch each other. I recommend not letting any shape touch more than 2 other shapes.

7. Be careful about accidently making letters. This can happen when blocks that contain narrow strips are touching other narrow panels of color. When arranging your blocks, step back to make sure you don't see Ts, Ls, or Fs forming.

Queen Sample layout

Twin Sample layout

SEWING IT TOGETHER

Once you are satisfied with the layout of the blocks, begin sewing the blocks in each column together. Take a photo of the blocks laid out before you start sewing, though, so you don't forget where each one goes.

While you piece, trim periodically, making sure all corners stay 90° and the shapes are neat and square. Once each column is formed, press the seams in the direction that makes the most sense to you, avoiding bulk.

Then, pin and sew the columns together. Press the seams to one side, and once all the columns are combined, square the quilt top so each corner is 90°. Hip hip hooray!

FINAL DIMENSIONS: 48˝ × 49˝

This type of improv technique uses all the colors and all the shapes. This is a great technique to use when the scrap-fabric bin is overflowing. In this technique, I use basic geometric shapes pieced intentionally to create organized chaos.

This technique is used to make The Stadium Quilt to Show Off at the Park (page 88), the Holiday Stockings (page 114), and the Organizing Pouches for Life (page 106).

Technique 3 sample quilt layout

CHOOSING FABRICS

Don't forget to check the Color Chart (page 21) for a key to the color abbreviations. When choosing your own colors, see Color and Balance (page 12). You could choose a whole bunch of colors or just a few. You're the boss, so you get to decide! You need a background (white or beige) for only 2 blocks: Checkerboard Block and Stripey Stripes Block.

Adding even the most subtly patterned fabric to this improv technique adds a visual texture that turns organized chaos into messy chaos. So, I recommend using only solids!

BUILDING BLOCKS

The "blocks" used in this technique are all rectangles of varying sizes.

Checkerboard Block
page 68

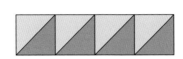

Half-Square Triangle (HST) Block
page 70

Stripey Stripes Block
page 71

TECHNIQUE 3 BLOCKS

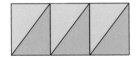

Half-Rectangle Triangle (HRT) Block
page 72

Three Stripe Block
page 73

Half-Circle Block
page 74

Two-Tone Block
page 74

Materials

Yardages are based on 42″ of usable width.

⅛ yard each of 6 colors (C, E, K, M, T, X)

¼ yard each of 3 colors (L, N, S)

⅓ yard each of 2 colors of (F, R)

⅛ yard of neutral background (W)

▶ HOLD UP!

The materials list here is just to get you started on each of the blocks—enough fabric to practice each block in this technique, but not enough to assemble into a project. These instructions will make 1 Checkerboard Block, 2 Half-Square Triangle Blocks, 1 Stripey Stripes Block, 2 Half-Rectangle Triangle Blocks, 3 Three Stripe Blocks, 1 Half-Circle Block, and 3 Two-Tone Blocks. Each project in the book has its own full materials list.

CHECKERBOARD BLOCK

Choose one color and the background color (W, E).

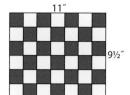

Cutting

| **You'll need:**

Fabric W

· 1 strip 2″ × WOF

Fabric E

· 1 strip 2″ × WOF

Stack and align the W and E yardage. Cut a strip 2″ × WOF from both colors.

Assembly

1. Pin and sew the 2 strips together along one long side. Press the seam allowance towards the darker color.

2. Cut the Step 1 unit into 3 equal parts. Measure the total length of the strips and divide by 3 to determine how far apart the cuts should be.

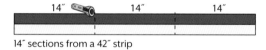

14″ sections from a 42″ strip

3. Pin and sew 2 Step 2 units together along one long side. Opposite color strips should touch. Press the seam allowance in the same direction as the first seam. Repeat to add on the third unit from Step 2. Trim to 14″ × 9½″.

4. With the stripes running horizontally, make vertical cuts 2″ apart. Depending on the original vertical width of the fabric, you should be able to make 5, 6, or 7 cuts. These units are now called strip squares—make 7 strip squares.

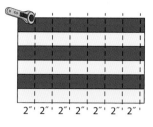

5. Flip every other strip 180°. Then, pair the strips next to one another, right sides together and opposite colors touching. 1 strip will be left over. Pin and sew the pairs along one long side to make 3 units.

6. Repeat Step 5 to combine the 3 units into 1 rectangle. Then, attach the seventh Strip Square to one side. Press all sems to the left. Trim to a 9½″ × 11″ rectangle.

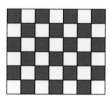

Variations and Use

An easy variation is to change the number of columns and use the extra as stripes. Use at least 4 Checkerboard Blocks (of different colors) in any quilt.

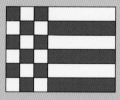

It's also easy to vary the square size. Instead of 2″ strips to start, make 2½″ or 1½″ strips, and then trim the columns to the same width.

HALF-SQUARE TRIANGLE BLOCK

These instructions will show you how to make 8 HSTs at a time to combine them into what I am calling a Half-Square Triangle Block. Choose 2 colors that you have at least ⅓ yard of (R, F).

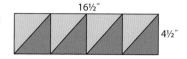

16½"

4½"

Cutting

You'll need:

Fabric R

· 1 square 10˝ × 10˝:

Subcut into 4 triangles

Fabric F

· 1 square 10˝ × 10˝

Subcut into 4 triangles

1. Stack and align the R and F yardage. Cut a 10˝ × 10˝ square from each color.

▶ PILE OF LONELY PANELS

All fabric scraps (not yardage) set aside during cutting should go into your Pile of Lonely Panels. Pull it out when you need it, or when I suggest it!

Assembly

1. Using a hera marker or other marking tool, mark an *X* on the fabric across both diagonals of the R square.

2. Stack and align the square from Step 1 with the F square. Sew a seam ¼˝ from one of the marked lines. Turn the block, and sewing back in the other direction, sew a second ¼˝ seam along the same line. Repeat with the second marked line.

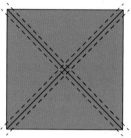

Two indented lines (solid) and 4 sewn lines (dashed)

3. Cut through the square 4 times, as shown (horizontal, vertical, on both marked lines).

4. Open up all 8 Half-Square Triangles (HSTs). Press all seams towards the same color. Trim so they are each 4½˝ × 4½˝.

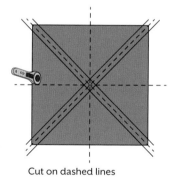

Cut on dashed lines

⫸ KEEPING SIZE CONSISTENT ⫷

If you have 1 HST that requires more than a little trimming and ends up smaller than the rest, don't sweat it. Just trim the rest of the HST Squares to those same smaller dimensions. What's most important is that the size is consistent between all of them.

5. Sew 4 of the HSTs together in a line with colors oriented the same way. Opposite colors should be touching as you align, pin (if needed), and sew. Repeat until you have 4 sewn together. Open and press seams to one side—whichever side feels less bulky. Repeat with the remaining 4 to make a second block.

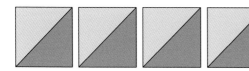

Variations and Use

My favorite variation on this block is when the 4 HSTs tell me they want to be a square instead of a line. Sew 2 pairs of HSTs, then combine the pairs into a square. Use at least 3 Half-Square Triangle Blocks in any quilt.

STRIPEY STRIPES BLOCK

This block is also used in Technique 1. To create it, follow the instructions in Stripey Stripes Block (page 31).

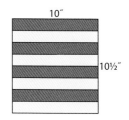

HALF-RECTANGLE TRIANGLE BLOCK

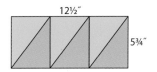

Choose 2 colors that you have at least ¼ yard of (S, L). Use at least 2 Half-Rectangle Triangle Blocks in any quilt.

Cutting

You'll need:

Fabric S

· 3 rectangles 7˝ × 5˝:

Subcut into 6 right triangles

Fabric L

· 3 rectangles 7˝ × 5˝:

Subcut into 6 right triangles

1. Stack and align the L and S yardage. Cut a 7˝ × WOF strip. Unfold and restack the strips. Subcut into 3 rectangles 7˝ × 5˝ of each color.

2. Stack the rectangles into 2 even piles. Cut from corner to corner on one diagonal across each stack.

Assembly

1. Pair an L triangle and an S triangle. Pin and sew along the hypotenuse. Press the seam toward the L triangle. Repeat to make 6 units. Trim each unit to 5¾˝ × 4½˝.

2. Sew the 3 units together in a line with colors oriented the same way. Trim to 12½˝ × 5¾˝.

THREE STRIPE BLOCK

Choose 3 colors (N, M, X). The instructions are written for ⅛ yardage, but this block particularly works well with scraps at least 2˝ × 14.˝

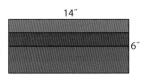

14˝

6˝

Cutting

You'll need:

Fabric N

· 2˝ × WOF

Fabric M

· 3˝ × WOF

Fabric X

· 2˝ × WOF

1. Stack and align the yardage of N and X. Cut a strip 2˝ × WOF.

2. Cut a strip 3˝ × WOF from the M yardage.

Assembly

1. Pin and sew the long side of any 2 strips together. Press the seam as desired.

2. Pin and sew the remaining strip onto the unit from Step 1 along any long side. The order of the strips doesn't matter. Press the seam in the same direction.

3. Cut the block into 3 rectangles about 14˝ long. The sweet spot for these blocks is between 12˝–16˝, so feel free to cut them anywhere within that range.

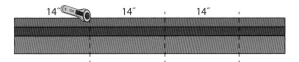

14˝   14˝   14˝

Variations and Use

You can easily vary the width of the strips—cut narrower or wider strips × WOF to start. You could also add more strips: what about a *Four Stripe Block*! Just don't let the total width of the block exceed 10˝.

Also vary the way you use the colors. Since you made 3 identical blocks via these instructions, consider how you'll use them to create balance or might want to shake up the next 3. Use about 6 Three Stripe Blocks in any quilt, but vary the colors and rotation.

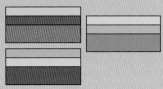

HALF-CIRCLE BLOCK

This block is also used in Technique 1. To create it, follow the instructions in Half-Circle Block (page 34). I used N and F fabric.

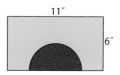

In addition to the variations on page 34, I like to cut the whole block in half vertically. In essence, making 2 identical Quarter-Circle Blocks. You could place them far apart in a quilt or rotate one and place them side by side.

TWO-TONE BLOCK

Use 2 tones of the same hue in this block (T,C). Maybe you choose cinnamon red and coral red, or mustard yellow and sunflower yellow. Scraps also work well for this block and allow you more color variation—you need pieces at least 2″ × 10.″

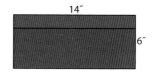

Cutting

You'll need:

Fabric C:

· 2″ × WOF

Fabric T:

· 4½″ × WOF

1. Cut a strip 2″ × WOF from the C yardage. Cut a strip 4½″ × WOF from the T yardage.

Assembly

1. Pin and sew the strips together along one long side.

2. Cut the block into 3 rectangles about 14″ long. The sweet spot for these blocks is between 12″–16″, so feel free to cut them anywhere within that range.

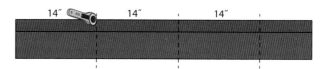

Variations and Use

Two-Tone Blocks can also vary in length and width. Cut different strips to start, or try making the blocks squarer by cutting different size rectangles.Use about 6 Two-Tone blocks in any quilts, with varied colors.

ASSEMBLING ALL THE BLOCKS

This is when the fun really begins. Puzzling each of your blocks is like finishing the world's most colorful Sudoku (without all the math).

If you've been following these instructions as written, you've only made a total of 13 blocks. Those were perfect Technique 3 Block practice, but, if you want to assemble them into a quilt, you'll need more blocks. Get sewing as your heart commands, or, you can follow along with the assembly technique here by checking out the sample quilt illustration. You can also check out The Stadium Quilt to Show Off at the Park (page 88), the Holiday Stockings (page 114), and the Organizing Pouches for Life (page 106) for more direction on how many and which kinds of blocks to make for a full-sized project.

The remaining steps for assembling Technique 3 blocks are the same as the assembly process for Technique 1, so first, read Assembling All the Blocks (page 35), then come back here for examples specific to Technique 3.

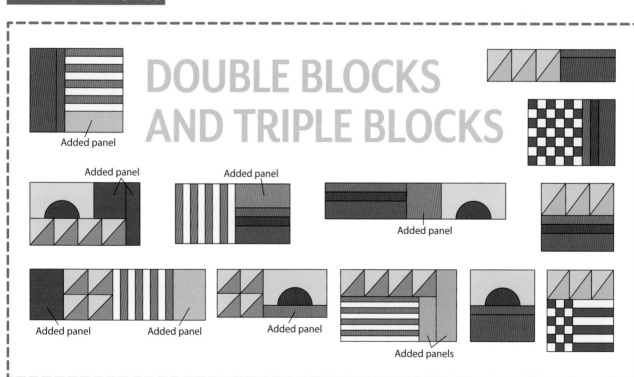

DOUBLE BLOCKS AND TRIPLE BLOCKS

Added panel

Added panel

Added panel

Added panel

Added panel

Added panel

Added panel

Added panels

In Example 1, the Checkerboard Block is too short on its own to sew onto the HST Block. So, sew a 9½˝ × 6˝ K rectangle panel onto the side of the Checkerboard Block first.

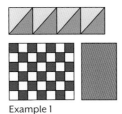

Example 1

You don't need to do the math to figure out the dimensions of the K rectangle panel. Just use the ruler to measure the approximate length of the gap the K panel will fill and round up, making the panel larger than it needs to be. Sew, and press the seam to the side. Then, attach the new Checkerboard Unit to the HST block. Trim off excess K panel.

In example 2, we want to pair a 5¾˝ HRT Block with a 6˝ × 14˝ Three Stripe Block, making the HRT block just 1½˝ too short. Instead of adding a small panel, let's trim the Three Stripe block.

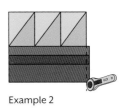

Example 2

Beware of trimming in weird places. For Half-Circle blocks, try to only make a vertical cut through the center. For HST and HRT Blocks, cut off whole shapes, not partial shapes. For the Checkerboard Block, cut off whole columns or rows, not partial squares.

⟨ MAKING STEPS WITH PANELS ⟩

Adding 2 panels of the same color to create a *step* is another way to add more length *and* visual dimension in a double block.

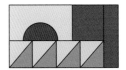

Two pink panels make a *step* in the middle of this technique 3 quilt.

▶ REMEMBER: THIS IS NOT A PATTERN

The hope is for you to use the general block shapes and forms in this chapter to learn to create your own improvised quilt... not just to be able to replicate these illustrations.

BIG
BLOCKS

Example layout from some of the example big blocks

Many, many colors in harmony on a Technique 3 quilt

PROJECTS

IMPROV TECHNIQUE 1 THROW QUILT
A Quilt to Impress Your Mother-In-Law

Imagine this scene: You are at your mother-in-law's 60th birthday bash. She is opening her presents: slippers, wine opener, hand lotion, another wine opener. Then she unwraps the present you made for her. *Made*, not bought. Her eyes glisten when she realizes you made her an improv quilt. "You made this *for me*...?" she starts to say before devolving into tears. Best. Present. Ever.

If you haven't read Technique 1: Classic Easy Improv (page 22), make sure you do that now. I refer back to that chapter frequently for this project. Remember, though this project gives you guidance for a full quilt, the goal is for you to catch your own wind and improv a similar project, not to copy the quilt exactly!

Materials

Yardages are based on 42″ of usable width.

Kona cotton solids (see chart)

Wool batting: 56″ × 72″

Half-Circle Inside and Outside Templates (page 11)

MIL FABRIC CHART

Kona cotton color	Amount Needed
Coral (C)	⅔ yard
Lingerie (G)	⅔ yard
Blueprint (H)	⅔ yard
Teal (E)	⅔ yard + 3¼ yards for backing
Terra Cotta (T)	⅔ yard
Snow (W)	⅔ yard
Foxglove (X)	⅔ yard
Chambray Linen (EE)	½ yard for binding

CUTTING AND PIECING

Technique 1: Building Blocks (page 24) gives instructions for how to make all of the blocks in this quilt. The chart (left) shows the Kona cotton fabric colors and amounts used in the sample quilt, though you might decide to use a different number of colors.

When cutting, I recommend going block-by-block instead of cutting for the whole quilt at once.

To start, cut and sew approximately 4–6 of each block. You may need to cut more later, or you may not use all of the shapes.

For the Final Mother-In-Law Quilt, I used 9 ABCBA Blocks, 6 Triangles Blocks, 6 Square in a Square Blocks, 4 Stripey Stripes Blocks, 4 Pd Blocks, 4 Half-Circle Blocks, and about 15 extra panels.

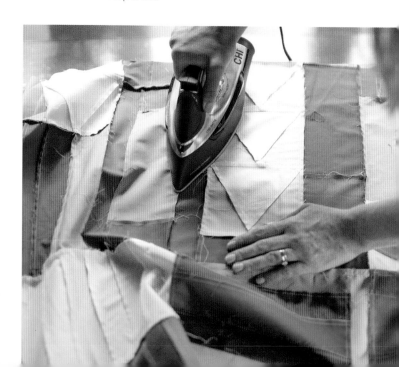

BLOCK VARIATIONS

Several variations of the standard blocks appear in the sample. These variations are included in the number of blocks listed on the previous page.

SQUARE IN A SQUARE BLOCK VARIATION: Dueling Square in a Square

Cutting List

Coral (C)

- 1 rectangle 2½″ × 6″
- 2 rectangles 2½″ × 5¼″

Teal (E)

- 1 rectangle 2½″ × 6″
- 2 rectangles 2½″ × 5¼″

Blueprint (H)

- 1 square 6″ × 6″

Instead of using 1 color for the interior square and 1 color for the exterior square, I used 2 colors for the exterior square. Sew this block by following the instructions for Square in a Square Block: Assembly (page 29). To make the side panels before Step 2, sew the C and E 5¼″ rectangles along the short edges into 2 pairs. Then attach them to the main unit.

SQUARE IN A SQUARE BLOCK VARIATION: Rectangle in a Rectangle

Cutting List

Foxglove (X)

- 1 rectangle 4″ × 9″

Terra Cotta (T)

- 2 squares 4″
- 2 rectangles 2½″ × 16″

Sew this block by following the instructions for Square in a Square Block: Assembly (page 29).

First, sew the squares to the short ends of the X rectangle. Then, attach the remaining rectangles to the other sides of the main unit. Trim to an 8″ × 16″ rectangle.

PD BLOCK VARIATION: Bigger Size

Cutting List

Coral (C)

- 1 rectangle 2½″ × 10½″
- 1 rectangle 4″ × 5½″

Terra Cotta (T)

- 1 rectangle 4½″ × 10½″
- 1 rectangle 4″ × 5½″

This variation just changes the size of the Pd Block. To cut and sew this block with the above dimensions, follow the instructions in Pd Block (page 33). Trim the block to 10″ × 10½″.

TRIANGLES BLOCK VARIATION: Two-Color Triangles

In this variation, the background color fabric is replaced with colorful fabric. I also only attached 2 triangles per block. For a cutting list, to cut, and to sew this block, follow the instructions in Triangles Block (page 26). Trim to 6½″ × 15″.

VARIATION 5: Bottomed-Out Half-Circle

Sew a 2½″ × 1″ rectangle to the bottom of the Half-Circle Block (page 34). The rectangle should be the same color as the exterior piece. Trim to an 8″ × 11″ rectangle.

ASSEMBLING THE QUILT TOP

To combine all of the blocks, see Assembling All the Blocks in Technique 1: Classic Easy Improv (page 35). Make sure that you're creating a balance of shape, scale, and texture. If you look closely at the Mother-In-Law Quilt (or the quilt illustration), you might be surprised by the number of extra panels I used. This is when the Pile of Lonely Panels (page 70) becomes the Pile of Happy Helpers!

Final quilt layout

FINISHING THE QUILT

Piece together the backing fabric to measure at least 56″ × 72″, or 4″ larger than your quilt top on all sides. Then, follow the instructions in How to Make a Quilt (page 16) to make the quilt sandwich, quilt, and bind the quilt. I made my binding from a ½ yard of EE cut into 6 strips 2½″ × WOF and pieced together.

Quilted by Molly Kohler using a custom straight-line custom design

IMPROV TECHNIQUE 3 THROW QUILT
A Stadium Quilt to Show Off at the Park

Do you want to know my favorite part about watching my preschool-age kids play recreational soccer? Is it the tiny shin guards and adorable team shirts? Is it the way their faces light up with pride when they get a touch on the ball? Okay yes, it is all of those things. But if I'm honest, my *favorite* favorite part of soccer Saturdays is the gasps of amazement I hear from the other parents when I lay down my improv quilt on the grassy sideline.

I bring this particular quilt to outdoor events because the backing has a water-resistant fabric that keeps at bay the moisture from wet grass or the particles of sand or dirt. When the event is over, simply wipe down the back of the quilt, fend off the hoards of quilty admirers, and fold it up for next time.

If you haven't read Technique 3: All the Colors, All the Shapes (page 64), make sure you do that now. I refer back to that chapter frequently for this project. Remember, though this project gives you guidance for a full quilt, the goal is for you to catch your own wind and improv a similar project, not to copy the sample exactly!

Materials

Yardages are based on 42″ of usable width.

Kona cotton solids (see chart)

Water-resistant backing fabric: 4 yards

Wool batting: at least 74″ × 72″

Half-Circle Inside and Outside templates (page 11)

STADIUM FABRIC CHART

Kona cotton color	Total Yardage Needed
Orangeade (AA)	⅓ yard
Cactus (BB)	⅓ yard
Pear (CC)	⅓ yard
Cornflower (F)	⅓ yard
Ice Peace (I)	⅓ yard
Sassy Pink (K)	⅓ yard + ½ yard for binding
Pansy (P)	⅓ yard
Grellow (Q)	⅓ yard
Sage (S)	⅓ yard
Terra Cotta (T)	⅓ yard
Copen (D)	¼ yard
Nectarine (J)	¼ yard
Pistachio (O)	⅛ yard
Bright Idea (V)	¼ yard
Snow (W)	¾ yard
Tricot swimwear fabric	3⅝ yards for backing

CHOOSING WATER-RESISTANT BACKING FABRIC

We have some options for the backing: oilcloth, Gore Tex, ripstop vinyl, laminated cotton, outdoor upholstery fabric, and other polyurethane-coated nylons or polyesters. Consider what level of water-resistance you need. Also, consider the latest research on textile chemicals. Most water-resistant fabrics contain per- and polyfluoroalkyl substances, also known as PFAS. These chemicals stay in fabrics indefinitely and can cause a host of health concerns when they are absorbed or breathed in. Checking fabric labels for the OEKO-TEX certification or explicit "non-flourinated fabric" statements will ensure no PFAS.

CUTTING AND PIECING

Technique 3: All the Colors, All the Shapes (page 64) gives instructions for how to make all of the blocks in this quilt. I also used the Triangles Block (page 26) from Technique 1, though note that as suggested by Triangles Block: Variations (page 28), I am only using 2 triangles in a row.

The chart (left) shows the Kona cotton fabric colors and amounts used in the sample quilt, though you might decide to use a different number of colors. When batch cutting, I recommend going block-by-block instead of cutting for the whole quilt at once.

To start, cut and sew approximately 4–6 of each block. You may need to cut more later, or you may not use all of the shapes.

For the Final Stadium Quilt, I used 4 Checkerboard Blocks, 4 Half-Square Triangle Blocks, 4 Triangles Blocks, 5 Stripey Stripes Blocks, 5 Half-Circle Blocks, 9 Two-Tone Blocks, 2 Half-Rectangle Triangle Blocks, about 15 Three Stripe Blocks, and about 10 extra panels.

BLOCK VARIATIONS

Several variations of the standard blocks appear in the sample. These variations are included in the number of blocks listed previously.

TWO-TONE BLOCK VARIATION: Thicker

Cutting List

Sage (S)

- 1 rectangle 4″ × 4½″

Pistachio (O)

- 1 rectangle 9″ × 4½″

Sew this block by following the instructions for Two-Tone Block (page 74). Trim to 4½″ × 12½″.

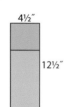

THREE-STRIPE BLOCKS BLOCK VARIATION: Thicker

Cutting List

Pink (K)

- 1 strip 2½″ × 10″

Terra Cotta (T)

- 1 strip 3½″ × 10″

Cactus (BB)

- 1 strip 5″ × 10″

Sew the rectangles together lengthwise to create a 10″ × 10″ square.

CHECKERBOARD BLOCK VARIATION: Change-Up

Just like in Checkerboard Block: Variations and Use (page 68), I varied the sizes of the Checkerboard Blocks. For a larger block, I used 2½″ × WOF strips to start. For a smaller block, I used 1¾″ × WOF strips to start. Instead of cutting the last two strip squares, I attached them as stripes.

STRIPEY STRIPES BLOCK VARIATION: Rainbow

Cutting List

Copen (D)

- 1 rectangle 2″ × 18″

Terra Cotta (T)

- 1 rectangle 2″ × 18″

Pink (K)

- 1 rectangle 1¾″ × 18″

Pansy (P)

- 1 rectangle 1¾″ × 18″

Ice Peach (I)

- 1 rectangle 2¼″ × 18″

Snow (W)

- 4 rectangles ½″ × 18″

Instead of using just 2 colors, I sometimes like making a whole rainbow of stripes! Sew this block by following the instructions in Stripey Stripes Block (page 31), alternating W and each color. Trim to 18″ × 11¾″.

TRIANGLES BLOCK VARIATION: Two-Color Triangles

In this variation, the background color fabric is replaced with colorful fabric. I also only attached 2 triangles per block. For a cutting list, to cut, and to sew this block, follow the instructions in Triangles Block (page 26). Trim to 6½″ × 15″.

ASSEMBLING THE DOUBLE BLOCKS AND BIGGER BLOCKS

To combine all the blocks, see Assembling All the Blocks in Technique 3: All the Colors, All the Shapes (page 75). Make sure that you're creating a balance of shape, scale, and texture.

Final quilt layout illustration

Notice the water-resistant backing

Quilted by Molly Kohler with a custom, straight-line custom design

FINISHING THE QUILT

ASSEMBLING IN STAGES

Because this is a *stadium* quilt with a water-resistant backing, we need to do things a little differently. When making stadium quilts, I like to quilt in 2 stages.

For Stage 1, sandwich and pin the quilt top and wool batting as normal. Quilt the top and wool batting together, just like any other quilting project (see How to Make a Quilt, page 16).

> ### ANOTHER POSSIBLE LAYER
> You could add a lightweight muslin as a backing fabric if you just don't want to topstitch a quilt sandwich that doesn't have 2 pieces of bread.

Now we add the water-resistant backing. I used Santorini Tricot swimwear fabric in Arctic Lime. The dimensions of my finished quilt top are 66″ × 63½″, so I pieced together the backing fabric to measure at least 74″ × 72″.

Lay the water-resistant backing on the floor, right side down. Stretch it out and secure the corners to the ground with tape. Place the quilted top and batting on top, right side up. Pin all 3 layers together. Then be judicious about how you sew it. Normally when quilting, I top stitch every couple inches, but here, I spread this out every couple feet. You don't want to perforate the waterproof backing too much. The batting won't be at risk of bunching, so this top stitching is really just to keep the backing fabric affixed.

Then, bind the quilt. I made my binding from a ½ yard of KK cut into 6 strips 2½″ × WOF and pieced together.

IMPROV TECHNIQUE 1 THROW QUILT
The (Not-Boring) Neutral Quilt

Using bright and unexpected colors in a quilt can bring delight and vibrancy and joy to a home. But using neutral and earthy hues in a quilt can bring comfort and versatility. Using neutral colors in a quilt need not be boring! In fact, subtle colors can be the perfect palette to showcase unique and intricate piecing designs. This is also the only project in the book for which I used patterned fabrics! Don't forget to check out Color and Balance (page 12) before you grab every patterned yard in your stash.

If you haven't read Technique 1: Classic Easy Improv (page 22), make sure you do that now. I refer back to that chapter frequently for this project. Remember, though this project gives you guidance for a full quilt, the goal is for you to catch your own wind and improv a similar project, not to copy the quilt exactly!

Materials

Yardages are based on 42˝ of usable width.

Kona cotton solids (see chart)

Wool batting: 76˝ × 62˝

Half-Circle Inside and Outside Templates
(page 11)

NEUTRAL FABRIC CHART

Kona cotton color	Total yardage Needed
Doeskin (DD)	¾ yard
Chambray Linen (EE)	¾ yard for piecing, 3½ yards for backing, ½ yard for binding
Sable (FF)	⅔ yard
Gotham Gray (GG)	1 yard
Diagonal Stripes (HH)	1 yard
Snow (W)	1 yard
Charcoal (Y)	½ yard

CUTTING AND PIECING

Technique 1: Building Blocks (page 24) gives instructions for how to make all of the blocks in this quilt. The chart (left) shows the Kona cotton fabric colors and amounts used in the sample quilt, though you might decide to use a different number of colors.

When batch cutting, I recommend going block-by-block instead of cutting for the whole quilt at once.

To start, cut and sew approximately 4–6 of each block. You may need to cut more later, or you may not use all of the shapes.

For the final Neutral Quilt, I used 4 Pd Blocks, 5 Shift Blocks, 5 Half-Circle Blocks, 5 Stripey Stripes Blocks, 6 Triangles Blocks, 6 Square in a Square Blocks, 6 ABCBA Blocks, and about 35 extra panels.

I make use of many W (background color) panels in this quilt. I often advise against using background color fabric as panels, but in an entirely neutral-colored quilt like this, I actually recommend it. In your own block assembling, you might find you use just as many or more panels in your assembly process. But don't worry if you use way fewer, too. That's the beauty of improv quilting: you are the boss!

BLOCK VARIATIONS

Several variations of the standard blocks appear in the sample. These variations are included in the number of blocks listed on the previous page.

Two variations I use here were already used in A Quilt to Impress Your Mother-In-Law. They are Square in a Square Block Variation: Rectangle in a Rectangle (page 85) and Pd Block Variation: Bigger Size (page 85).

TRIANGLES BLOCK VARIATION: Mismatched

Cutting List

Chambray (EE)

· 2 equilateral 60° triangles, 5¼˝ tall, 6˝ on all sides

· 4 right triangles 4˝ × 7˝

· 2 rectangles 2˝ × 6½˝

Charcoal (Y)

· 2 equilateral 60° triangles, 5¼˝ tall, 6˝ on all sides

· 4 right triangles 4˝ × 7˝

· 2 rectangles 2˝ × 6½˝

This variation combines several changes: replacing the background color and mix-and-matching the triangle colors into pairs. I also added a rectangular panel to the bottom of each triangle.

To piece this variation with the above pieces and extra 2˝ × 6½˝ rectangles, follow the instructions in Triangles Blocks (page 26). Piece the individual triangle squares (after Step 5) to the rectangles. The corner cut-offs from making the equilateral triangles are used in the Whirligig variation for this project. Save them!

HALF-CIRCLE BLOCK VARIATION: Whirligigs

Cutting List

Doeskin (DD)

· 1 half-circle from Half-Circle Outside Template

· 1 rectangle 2½˝ × 1˝

Charcoal (Y)

· 3 right triangles 3½˝ × 6˝ (cut offs from Triangles Block)

Snow (W)

· 3 right triangles 3½˝ × 6˝ (cut offs from Triangles Block)

1. Place a Y triangle on top of a W triangle, right sides together. Line up the points of the smallest angle. Pin along the right side. Sew. Press that seam to the left. Repeat to make 3 pairs of W and Y triangles.

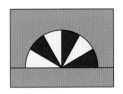

2. Sew the pairs together, alternating the colors. Don't worry too much about getting perfect points at the center. Trim to the size of the Half-Circle Inside Template, aligning the center points.

3. Follow Half-Circle Block: Assembly (page 34) to attach the units from Steps 1–2. Sew the 2½˝ × 1˝ rectangle to the bottom of the block.

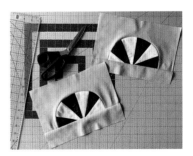

ASSEMBLING THE DOUBLE BLOCKS AND BIGGER BLOCKS

To combine all the blocks, see Assembling All the Blocks in Technique 1: (page 35). Make sure that you're creating a balance of shape, scale, and texture. If you look closely in the sample quilt, you might be surprised by the number of extra panels I used. This is when the Pile of Lonely Panels becomes the Pile of Happy Helpers!

Final quilt layout illustration

FINISHING THE QUILT

Piece together the backing fabric to measure 76˝ × 62˝, or 4˝ larger than your quilt top on all sides. Then, follow the instructions in How to Make a Quilt (page 16) to make the quilt sandwich, quilt, and bind the quilt. I made my binding from a ½ yard of EE cut into 7 strips 2½˝ × WOF and pieced together.

Quilted by Janet Hollandsworth with a Modern Curves pattern

IMPROV TECHNIQUE 2 TWIN QUILT
Duochrome Bed Quilt

Making bed-sized quilts can be intimidating, amiright? Big quilts have, traditionally, required a commitment of time and resources that aren't for the faint of heart. But not so with the Duochrome bed quilt. This is the fastest, funnest bed quilt you'll ever forge. Fashioning with only 2 colors frees you from the fatigue of fabric finding. Just pick your 2 happiest hues and you're set!

If you haven't read Technique 2: Sparse and Geometric (page 46), make sure you do that now. I refer back to that chapter frequently for this project. Remember, though this project gives you guidance for a full quilt, the goal is for you to catch your own wind and improv a similar project, not to copy the sample exactly!

Materials

Yardages are based on 42˝ of usable width.

2 Kona cotton solids (see chart)

Wool batting: 79˝ × 96˝

Quarter Round Square Templates and
Round Rectangle Templates (page 11)

DUOCHROME FABRIC CHART

Kona cotton color	Total Yardage Needed
Bluegrass (JJ)	4 yards
Pickle (L)	3 yards for piecing ⅝ yard for binding
Blueprint (H)	5½ yards for backing fabric

CUTTING AND PIECING

Technique 2: Building Blocks (page 50) gives
instructions for how to make all of the blocks in this
quilt. I am only using 2 colors, but remember you're
the boss, and you can always use more!

To start, choose which of the Technique
2 blocks you want to make. Then cut and sew
9 blocks 24˝ × 24˝ square and 3 rectangle blocks
18˝ × 24˝. Refer to the Block Layouts (page 48) for the
twin quilt.

For the final Duochrome Quilt, I used 1 of each of
the following Blocks: Quarter Round Square Block,
ET Square Block, Round Rectangle Block, Big Bubba
Square Block, Little Corner Square Block, and Partial
Line Square Block. I used 2 of each of the following
blocks: HST Square Block, Slope Square Block and
Power Rectangle.

ASSEMBLING THE SQUARE BLOCKS AND RECTANGLE BLOCKS

When assembling this quilt,
remember that though each
column needs 3 squares and
1 rectangle, you can place the
rectangle anywhere within each
column. For guidance assembling
and arranging the blocks, see
Technique 2: Assembling All the
Blocks (page 61).

Since this is a 2 color quilt,
additionally consider where
2 pieces of the same color are
touching among multiple blocks. You don't want to create
undesirable shapes when combining blocks!

71˝		
24˝ × 24˝	24˝ × 24˝	24˝ × 24˝
24˝ × 24˝	24˝ × 24˝	24˝ × 24˝
24˝ × 24˝	24˝ × 24˝	24˝ × 24˝
18˝ × 24˝	18˝ × 24˝	18˝ × 24˝

88½˝

Technique 2 twin quilt layout

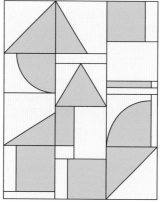

Undesirable, blobby shapes from
the same color touching too much.

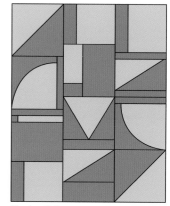

Final quilt layout

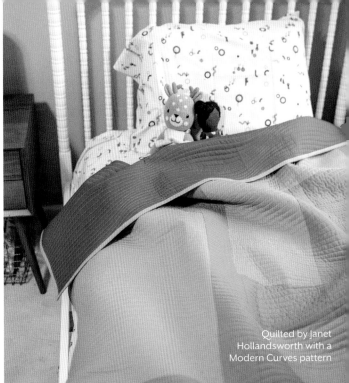

Quilted by Janet Hollandsworth with a Modern Curves pattern

FINISHING THE QUILT

Piece together the backing fabric to measure 79˝ × 96˝ (about 4˝ larger than the quilt top on each side). Then, follow the instructions in How to Make a Quilt (page 16) to make the quilt sandwich, quilt, and bind the quilt. I made my binding from a ⅝ yard of L cut into 9 strips 2½˝ × WOF and pieced together.

IMPROV TECHNIQUE 3 BAG
Organizing Pouches for Life

My own family's uses of Organizing Pouches for Life include, but are not limited to:

· a pouch for carrying my son's Type One Diabetes supplies

· a pouch to hold Mom's car snacks (the good candy that I do not share with the children)

· a pouch for transporting sandy goggles and sunscreen home from the beach

· a first aid supply pouch to keep in the back of the van

· a library books pouch to make sure we don't lose any (spoiler: we still do)

· a pouch for the pouches within the pouches to pouch

Share your makes with #organizingpouchesforlife

YARDAGE AND CHOOSING FABRICS

One thing that makes these organizing pouches so versatile is their water-resistant lining. Read Choosing Water-Resistant Backing Fabric (page 90).

Choosing materials for the outside of the bag can be as simple as using whatever solid fabrics you have on hand! Using scrap fabrics, though, could feel constraining. Maybe there aren't enough scraps to make the full block exactly to the color and size specifications instructed. Though this is the perfect opportunity to improv, if using scraps adds more stress, you can always pull out fabric yardage and cut fresh pieces to make Technique 3 blocks.

If you do want to use fabric yardage, a fat eighth of 13 colors (BB, C, F, H, II, KK, L, N, O, R, S, T, W), and a ¼ yard of 2 colors (X, P) will be the right amount. The color scheme for this project is all of the colors.

▶ FAT WHAT NOW?

A "fat quarter" is, like it sounds, a quarter of a yard of fabric. But it is measured in a special way: 18˝ × 22˝. Similarly, "fat eighths" are cut 9˝ × 22˝. quarters and fat eighths are available for purchase at most fabric shops.

For batting, I suggest a low loft cotton or bamboo.

MAKING THE TEMPLATE

Tape together pieces of paper
or cardstock to create a rectangle 21¼″ × 11″.
Draw a diagonal line across the top 4¼″
of the paper. This is the Organizing Pouch
Template!

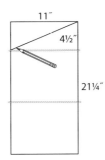

CUTTING AND PIECING THE EXTERIOR

Technique 3: All the Colors, All the Shapes (page 64) gives instructions
for how to make all of the blocks in this project. The ones that I
especially like to use when piecing the outside of an organizing pouch
are: Checkerboard Block, Half-Square Triangle Blocks, Stripey Stripes
Block, Half-Rectangle Triangle (HRT) Block, and Three Stripe Block.

Following instructions in Technique 3: All the Colors, All the Shapes
(page 64), make 3–5 total blocks. Keep in mind, because the organizing
pouches are so much smaller than a quilt, try out smaller variations of
the blocks.

Once you've completed the blocks, it's time to make a teeny tiny
quilt top. Assemble the blocks, keeping in mind Assembling All the
Blocks in Technique 3: All the Colors, All the Shapes (page 75) and
adding panels or trimming blocks as necessary. Aim for a final rectangle
around 24″ × 36.″ This might be enough for 2 whole pouches, but even
if I'm making just one, it gives me plenty of room to work.

Example mini quilt layout

THE LEAN

If you want the shapes on the exterior of your pouch to follow typical grid lines, you could (because you are the boss) create your pouch without a lean. The lean, however, reduces the need to carefully create balance of shapes and colors because the balance is purposefully off-kilter. It also forgivingly hides any edges that aren't perfectly parallel.

Line up the teeny tiny quilt top so it is square with the cutting mat. Place the Organizing Pouch

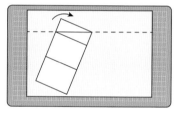

Template you made on top, parallel to the quilt top. Tilt the template so that the diagonal line is running parallel to the horizontal cutting mat lines. Using the water-soluble marker, draw the outline of the template onto the quilt top. Cut out.

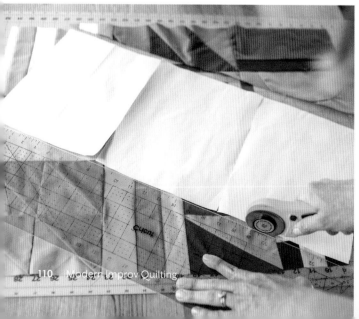

QUILTING THE POUCH EXTERIOR

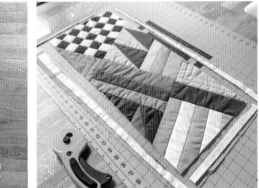

Quilted sandwich with cotton lining

1. Lay out a piece of batting around 24˝ × 15,˝ slightly larger than the exterior. Stack the zipper pouch exterior on top, right side up. If you're using cotton fabric for the interior of the pouch, place a 24˝ × 15˝ rectangle underneath the batting, right side down, to complete the sandwich. If you're using water resistant fabric, keep that set aside for now. Smooth and pin baste the (2 or 3) layers together.

2. Using the walking foot, quilt the sandwich however you want to! Straight lines, a grid pattern, free motion or "stitch in the ditch" all work well for this project. Then trim the extra batting from the sides so the mini quilt is once again 21¼˝ × 11˝.

3. Optional: If you are using water-resistant interior fabric, attach it now with a few pins. Quilt the sandwich again, this time using just a handful of stitch lines. The more stitching, the less water-resistant it will be. Trim excess material.

ASSEMBLING THE POUCH

1. Lay the quilted exterior right side up. Place the zipper face down along the top, short edge, with the zipper pull toward the left. Using the zipper foot, sew along the outer edge of the zipper.

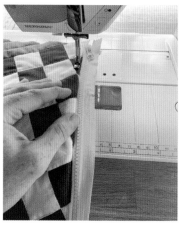

2. Flip the zipper over to face up. Press the seam toward the fabric, being careful not to melt water-resistant lining. Topstitch along the right side of the seam, about ¼˝ from the zipper.

3. Fold the rectangle in half, right sides together, moving the bottom short side to meet the zipper at the top. Pin in place, right side of zipper to right side of pouch exterior. Stitch the second side of the zipper to the unattached side of the pouch.

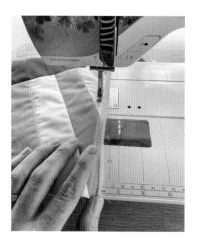

4. Repeat Step 2 on the second side. Unzip the zipper before sewing the second line of stitches.

5. Close the zipper, and turn the pouch right side out. Fold the pouch over about 1½˝ so that the zipper is part of the way down the front, as shown. When you've found where you want the fold to be, create it with your fingers, then press it with an iron. Mark the fold with a pin on each side.

6. Flip the pouch inside out. Crease the fold on the inside, and unzip the zipper at least halfway. Use binder clips to secure the fold. Using the walking foot, sew the sides of the pouch closed with a ¼˝ seam allowance. Backstitch, and sew carefully over the 2 ends of the zipper.

10. Turn the pouch right side out. Push out the corners, and press.

IMPROV TECHNIQUE 3 STOCKINGS
Cheery Holiday Stockings

Here in Michigan, winter is cold and dark and lasts forever. (Why do we live here?) So, we must find the little things that bring brightness: sledding down slick slopes, winking twinkle lights, hot chocolate with marshmallows, and cheery stockings. My family's stockings help us celebrate Christmas and are placed under the nativity scene and garland on the mantel. Whether you celebrate Christmas or Hannukah or Kwanzaa, there is nothing like a bright stocking full of candy and gifts to add a little cheer to the holiday season. This chapter provides instructions to make 2 stockings. Share your makes with **#cheeryholidaystocking**

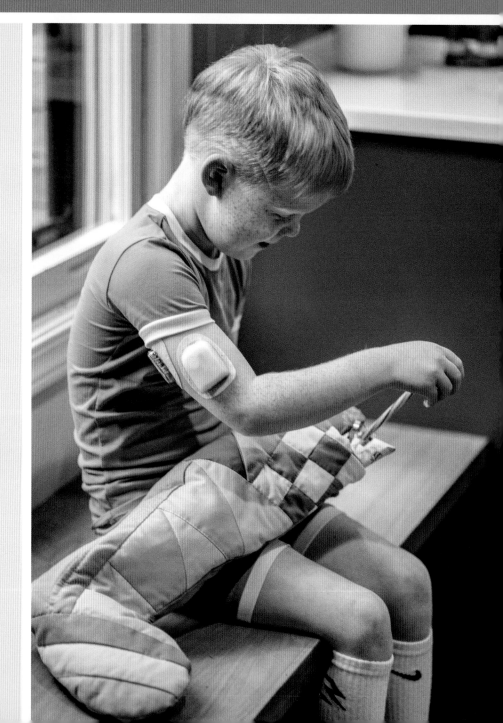

Materials

Yardages are based on 42″ of usable width.

Batting: 2 fat quarters, or ½ yard

Kona cotton solid scraps (see right)

Cotton backing fabric: 2 fat quarters, or ½ yard

Lining fabric: 1 yard

Batting: 22″ × 15″

2½″ × 12″ rectangle for hanging tag

Stocking Template (page 11)

Half-Circle Templates if using curved blocks (optional) (page 11)

CHOOSING MATERIALS

Pick whatever fabric yardage you like for the back. Maybe now is when you would love to use a patterned Christmas fabric (as long as there are no puppies in Santa suits on it—we've got to draw the line somewhere). For the lining, I highly recommend using a solid color that doesn't have a "right side" and "wrong side."

Scrap fabrics are perfect for making the front of the stockings. Using scrap fabrics for this project could feel constraining. Maybe there aren't enough scraps to make the full block exactly to the color and size specifications instructed. Though this is the perfect opportunity to improv, if using scraps adds more stress, you can always pull out fabric yardage and cut fresh pieces to make Technique 3 blocks.

If you do want to use fabric yardage, a fat eighth of 15 colors, and a fat quarter of 3 colors will be the right amount. I do not recommend trying to limit the palette. I am using fat eighths of B, BB, C, F, II, K, L, LL, O, Q, R, S, T, U, and W. I'm using fat quarters of H, P, and X.

▶ FAT WHAT NOW?

A "fat quarter" is, like it sounds, a quarter of a yard of fabric. But it is measured in a special way: 18″ × 22″. Similarly, "fat eighths" are cut 9″ × 22″. Fat quarters and fat eighths are available for purchase at most fabric shops.

Finally, for the tag, you could use a narrow piece of sewable leather, another cotton fabric scrap, or even a measure of elastic left over from all those face masks you sewed back in 2020.

THE TAG

Fold the rectangle in half like a hot dog bun. Press. Open the fold, then using the crease as a guide, fold in the raw edges to meet in the middle. Press again. Fold along the first line again, sealing the raw edges inside. Sew a line of stitching along the open edge. Cut into 2 pieces 6″ long.

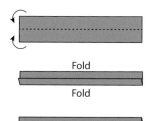

Fold

Fold

CUTTING AND PIECING THE FRONT

Technique 3: All the Colors, All the Shapes (page 64) gives instructions for how to make all of the blocks in this project. The ones that I especially like to use when piecing the Stocking fronts are: Checkerboard Block, Half-Square Triangle Block, Stripey Stripes Block, Half-Rectangle Triangle (HRT) Block, and Three Stripe Block.

Following instructions in Technique 3: All the Colors, All the Shapes (page 64), make 8–10 total blocks. Because the stockings are so much smaller than a quilt, try out smaller variations of the blocks.

Once you've completed the blocks, it's time to make a teeny tiny quilt top. Assemble the blocks,

keeping in mind Assembling All the Blocks in Technique 3: All the Colors, All the Shapes (page 75) and adding panels or trimming blocks as necessary.

Sample mini quilt layout for stockings

THE LEAN

If you want the shapes on the stocking to follow typical grid lines, you could (because you are the boss) cut the stocking shape without a lean. The lean, however, reduces the need to carefully create balance of shapes and colors because the balance is purposefully off-kilter. It also forgivingly hides any edges that aren't perfectly parallel.

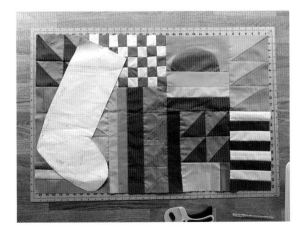

Line up the teeny tiny quilt top so it is square with the cutting mat. Place the paper Stocking Template on top, parallel to the quilt top. Tilt the template so that the pattern line is running parallel to the horizontal cutting mat lines. Using

the water-soluble marker, draw the outline of the template onto the quilt top. Cut out.

Then, move the Stocking Template over and cut a second stocking. If there's not enough room, cut a partial stocking, as large as possible. Then, sew on a block, a partial block, or the remainder of the mini quilt rectangle to the partial stocking. Tilt and match the block orientations. Position the template back on top of the second stocking, and cut away the excess.

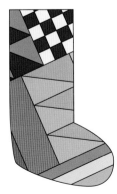

STOCKING CONSTRUCTION

Complete all following instructions for both stockings.

QUILTING THE STOCKING EXTERIOR

1. Lay out a piece of batting around 22″ × 15,″ slightly larger than the exterior of the stocking. Trim to be about 1″ larger than the exterior on all sides. Stack the stocking on top, right side up. Baste together with pins.

2. Using a walking foot, quilt the exterior and batting. Straight lines, a grid pattern, free motion, or "stitch in the ditch" all work well for this project. Then trim the extra batting from the sides.

ASSEMBLING THE STOCKING

1. Using the Stocking Template, cut out the back of the stocking from the yardage of your preferred fabric. If you are using a printed fabric, make sure your fabric is facing down on the cutting service before you use the template. Then use the template to cut out 2 stockings from the lining fabric.

2. Lay out the stocking pieces as shown. Fold the 6″ hanging tag in half, and pin it to the back exterior piece, with the ends of the tag aligned with the top of the stocking and at least ¼″ from the corner. Finally, stack the lining pieces on top of the exterior pieces, right sides together. Pin.

3. Sew the top edges of both pairs. Press the seams open. Open the stockings up.

4. Stack the 2 pairs, right sides together and linings aligned, and pin all the way around the exterior, leaving a small 3″- 4″ gap at the heel of the lining side.

◀ TAG TIP ▶

Make sure the hanging tag is tucked out of the way. You don't want to sew over any part of that tag when you stitch the pairs together.

5. Starting at the toe side of the lining, sew all the way around the perimeter of the stockings, leaving that gap unsewn.

6. Reach inside the stockings from the gap you left and grab the toe on the other side. Pull it, turning the whole stocking right side out. Push out all corners and curves. With your fingers and iron, fold and press the remaining gap in the heel of the lining in about ½˝. Clip or pin the folded gap closed. Sew closed with a topstitch.

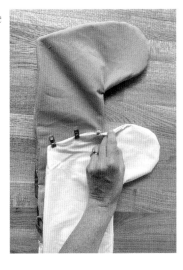

7. Push the lining fabric into the exterior of the stocking. Align the shapes, and press to smooth out any wrinkles. Repeat the assembly process with the other stocking exterior. Hang those stockings on the mantel and celebrate!

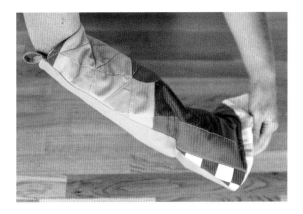

IMPROV TECHNIQUE 2 BAG
The Get Going Duffle

All of my little kids love to pack. Weeks before a camping trip, they will ask, "Can we start packing the car?" Then they'll shove every single one of their stuffed animals and just one pair of pants into a duffle bag. Despite vacation being weeks away, they want to get going. I, too, love the anticipation that comes with packing a bag, knowing everything I need for the next three days will be right there, snug and secure. So when I set out to create this duffle bag, I knew it had to be both joyful and practical, a bag that would help people of all ages get going. Share your makes with **#getgoingduffle**

Materials

Yardages are based on 42" of usable width.

Kona cotton solids (see right)

Cotton lining fabric: 1¼ yards

Canvas fabric: 10" × 20" rectangle (about ¼ yard)

Kona Lingerie (G) fabric (for binding): ¼ yard

25" size #5 zipper

1½" heavy polypropylene webbing: 4¾ yards for strapping and tabs

2 lobster clasps with 1½" oval rings

Nickel D rings (1½")

Wool batting: 1½ yards

Duffle Bag End Template (page 11)

CHOOSING MATERIALS

The outside and the inside of the duffle are primarily quilting cotton. Choose a high-quality cotton that will withstand being tossed around in an airplane luggage compartment. I prefer wool batting for the duffle bag because it is lofty and sturdy. Choose plastic zippers. Trust me on this. Metal-toothed zippers are heavy and hard to trim.

While I usually advocate for using scraps on bag projects, for Mrs. Duffleupagus, you probably need yardage. Know that I am doubly impressed by any attempts at using scraps first.

So, you need ⅛ yard of 6 colors (C, G, L, N, O, S), ⅓ yard of 1 color (K), ½ yard of 4 colors (CC, E, II, M), ¾ yard of 2 colors (F, X), and ⅘ yard of 1 color (T).

One final note on the polypropylene webbing: This material can sometimes be slippery and hard to secure with stitches when used to make the bag tabs. So, before inserting the tabs, I recommend using a wand lighter to slightly burn the ends of each tab. If you want to avoid this altogether, feel free to use cotton webbing instead.

CUTTING AND PIECING

For this project, we'll use several Technique 2: Sparse, Geometric Improv (page 46) blocks. I like the Slope Square Block, the Equilateral Triangle (ET) Square Block, and the Half-Square Triangle (HST) Square Block. We'll also use one Technique 3: All the Colors, All the Shapes (page 64) block, the Checkerboard Block. Remember though, you can choose whichever square and rectangle blocks you want! Catch your improv wave.

Cut and piece 3 square 24" × 24" blocks, and 2 Checkerboard blocks 9½" × 11."

▶ ET BLOCK VARIATION

I use a variation of the ET block in this duffel. Do not add the 3½" × 24" to the top of the ET block. This means that this block is not actually square.

CUTTING BAG PIECES AND CONSTRUCTION OVERVIEW

Mrs. Duffleupagus is made of 3 rectangular shapes (the body and 2 side pockets) and 2 arch shapes (for the 2 ends).

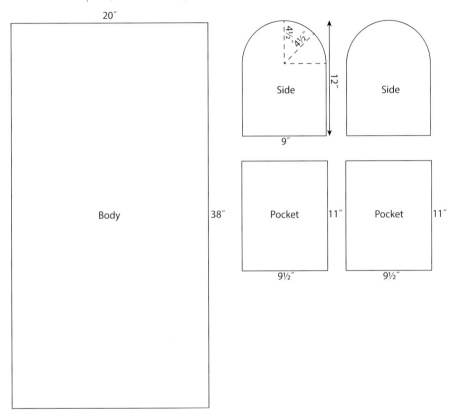

THE BODY

Piece together the 2 square 24″ × 24″ blocks (Slope Square Block and ET Blocks) as shown. Then, trim to square the rectangle down to 20″ × 38″. You can trim all off of 2 sides, or distribute it across all 4 sides. I recommend trimming the 24″ side equally from both edges.

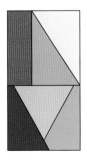

THE POCKETS

Finished 9½″ × 11″ Checkerboard Blocks (page 68)

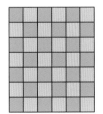

THE ENDS

I am using HST Square Blocks for the ends of the bag. Cut the HST Square into quarters (making 4 squares 12″ × 12″). Set aside the solid colored squares. Trim 3″ off one side of the remaining 2 squares, making them 9″ × 12″ rectangles.

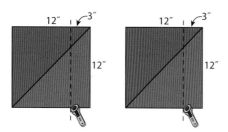

Cut out the Duffle Bag End template and trace it onto the 9″ × 12″ rectangle with a water-soluble marker. Finally, cut on the line you traced to make the top into an arch and the bottom corners rounded.

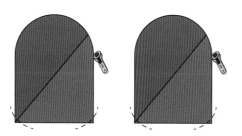

REMAINING CUTTING LIST
This table shows the remaining shapes you need to cut for binding.

Fabric—Piece	Cut
Pickle (L)—Pocket Binding	1 strip 2½″ × WOF
Pistachio (O)—Body Binding	1 strip 2½″ × WOF
Lingerie (G)—Interior Binding	3 strips 2½″ × WOF

LINING FABRIC AND BATTING

For my lining of the main body, I am using a fun Kelly Ventura print fabric, but solids work well, too. From the 1¼ yards, cut 1 rectangle 24″ × 43″ and 2 rectangles 14″ × 11.″ Repeat, cutting the same shapes from the batting.

For the pockets, find 2 scraps of fabric and 2 scraps of batting and trim to 12″ × 13″.

QUILTING THE PARTS

Now let's get quilting! Layer, baste, and quilt the following quilt sandwiches. Remember the fabric on top (listed first) is facing right side up. The fabric on the bottom (listed last) is facing right side down. When you are finished quilting each piece, give it a press and trim off the excess batting and back so the dimensions are once again the dimensions of the top, listed below (unless otherwise noted)

- The Body: 20˝ × 38˝ body piece / 24˝ × 43˝ batting / 24˝ × 43˝ lining fabric

- The Pockets (× 2): 9½˝ × 11˝ Checkerboard Block / 11˝ × 13˝ batting / 12˝ × 13˝ lining fabric

- The Ends (× 2): 9˝ × 12˝ Arched HST / 11˝ × 14˝ batting / 11˝ × 14˝ lining fabric

ASSEMBLY

BINDING POCKET EDGES

Use the 2½˝ × WOF L binding strip to bind the top edge of both Checkerboard pockets, For each pocket:

1. Fold the L strip in half lengthwise and press. Pin both raw edges of the binding to the top of the pocket. The right side of the binding should face the wrong side of the pocket. Sew. Trim the excess binding off of each side.

Fold

2. Turn the folded part of the binding over to the front of the pocket. Press and clip or pin in place. Sew the binding to the front of the pocket, as close to the edge of the fold as possible.

Sew.

BINDING MAIN BODY EDGES

Repeat Steps 1–2 from Binding Pocket Edges (above) to bind both 20˝ edges of the body piece with the 2½˝ × WOF O binding strip.

ATTACHING POCKETS

1. Find the center point of each short edge of the main body. From that point, measure 4˝ towards the center of the rectangle and mark with a pin. Place the bound tops of the checkerboard pockets in alignment with the pins, right side facing up. Center it between the long edges. Pin in place.

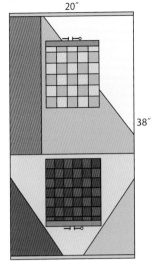

20˝

38˝

2. Sew around 3 sides of each pocket, leaving the bound edge unsewn.

ATTACHING STRAPS

1. Cut a piece of the strapping 3½ yards and fold in half to find the center (63˝ on each side). Put a pin in the center. Mark the center of the main body piece, between the pockets, with the hera marker, about 19˝ from the top short edge.

2. Place the center of the strapping on the center of the main body piece, with the strap running in the same direction as the body piece. Scoot the strap over until it overlaps with the edges of the pockets by ½˝ and pin.

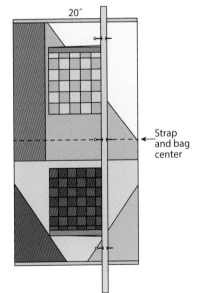

20˝

Strap and bag center

3. Fold each end of the strapping in a loop, back towards the bag, with the ends meeting again in the center of the main body. Make sure the strap doesn't twist, and overlap the other side of the pockets by ½˝. Pin.

4. Sew down the straps by stitching around both edges of the straps, but only from the top edge of one pocket to the top edge of the other pocket. Repeat on both sides. The stitch line should be about ¼˝ from the edges.

Reinforce the strap at the 4 corners. Back stitch several times, or add a triangle of stitching for security. Where the 2 ends of the straps meet in the center of the main body, sew zig-zag stitches back and forth to reinforce the connection.

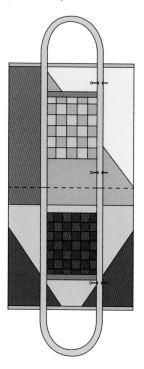

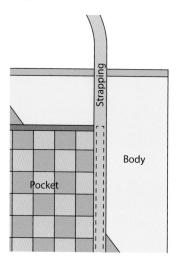

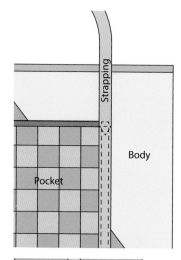

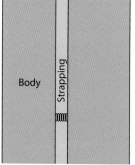

Reinforced stitching where the two strap ends connect

ATTACHING CANVAS BOTTOM

1. Fold both of the long edges of the 10˝ × 20˝ canvas rectangle in toward the wrong side by 1˝. Press.

2. Place the canvas right side up on the right side of the main body piece, horizontally. Pin in place.

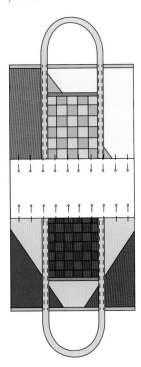

3. Sew along both long edges of the canvas, as close to the fold as possible.

ATTACHING MAIN ZIPPER

1. Fold both short (bound) edges of the main body bag in towards the center, wrong sides together. Lay the closed zipper, facing up, in between the bound edges. Using clips or pins, attach the zipper to one side of the binding. The zipper should be underneath the binding. Align the pull of the zipper with the top of the body. The stop end of the zipper should overhang at the bottom of the body.

2. With the zipper foot, sew the zipper and one side of the binding together. Sew ⅛˝ from the edge of the binding.

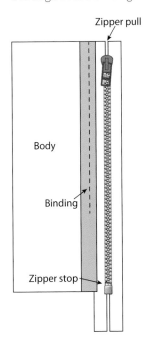

3. Unzip the zipper. Line up the other side of the zipper with the other side of the binding and pin or clip. Repeat Step 2 to sew the other side of the zipper to the other edge of binding. This time, start on the opposite side of the unzipped zipper pull.

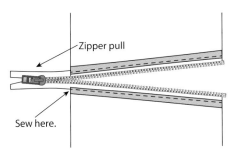

4. Zip the zipper. Trim off the excess zipper that is beyond the body of the bag.

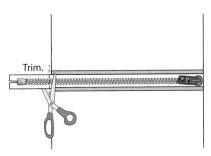

ATTACHING TABS

1. Cut 2 pieces of webbing each 4″ long. Run a D ring onto both pieces, then fold the webbing strips in half. These are tabs.

2. Clip or pin the unfolded edges of each tab to each end of the main zipper at the edges of the bag. The ring should face in towards the center of the bag. Using the walking foot, sew the tab to the zipper and bag. Slow the stitching when going over the teeth. Sew back and forth a couple times to strengthen the seam.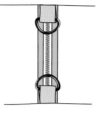

MAKING SHOULDER STRAP

1. Thread one end of the remaining 1 yard of webbing through the opening of the swivel clip. Pull through about 2″ of the end. Fold ½″ of that end, and pin in place. Using the zipper foot, sew back and forth on the fold, securing it.

2. Repeat Step 1 with the other side of the strap and the second swivel clip.

FINAL ASSEMBLY

1. Unzip the main zipper a few inches and flip the body inside out. Tuck the straps in toward the center. Line up the top center (right side facing in) of an 9″ × 12″ arched end panel with the zipper on the main body. Clip together all the way around. Repeat with the second end panel on the other side of the bag.

2. Sewing very slowly with a walking foot, sew all the way around both  end panels. It's okay if the seam is slightly larger than ¼.″

INTERIOR BINDING AND FINISHING

This last step is just for aesthetics. I don't mind leaving my inside duffle seams unbound, but it does add a dash of polish.

1. Piece together the 3 G 2½˝ × WOF strips. See Bind the Edges (page 19) for a reminder on binding strips. Fold in half longways, and press.

2. With the bag still inside out, find an end panel seam. Fold the raw short edge of the binding in ½˝, and then pin to the seam. Sew the raw edge of the binding to the seam, with the fold facing the panel interior.

❚ MATCHING THE STITCHING LINE ❚
As you sew the binding on, try to match the ¼˝ seam you made when you sewed the end panel and body together. This will help the bag maintain the shape you already sewed.

3. When you get back to where you started, keep sewing ½˝ over the existing binding. Cut off the excess binding.

4. Turn the folded edge of the binding over to the other side of the seam, encasing it. Clip in place. Sew down along the folded edge. Don't worry about sewing close to the fold this time.

5. Repeat Steps 1–4 for all interior seams. Flip the bag right side out.

Cross Body Wonder Bag

When you wear your Cross Body Wonder Bag, get ready for people to wonder: "Where did you *get* that?!" "How did you *make* that?!" "You can wear it around your *waist*, too?!" and "Will you make *me* one?!" Share your makes with **#crossbodywonderbag**

CHOOSING MATERIALS

The outside and the inside of the cross-body wonder bag are made of high-quality quilting cotton and sturdy wool batting. I use plastic zippers because I find them easy to sew with and smooth to zip in daily use

This project is perfect for using scraps. If you need to buy yardage, a fat eighth of 4 colors (D, II, GG, S), a quarter yard of 6 colors (E, K, L, N, T, X), and ⅓ yard of 1 color (G) will be the right amount. Instead of a uniform lining color, I'm using scraps for the lining pieces.

Refer to the Crossbody Cutting Chart (at right) before completing this section.

CUTTING AND PIECING

For this project, you only need 1 block from Technique 3: All the Colors, All the Shapes (page 64), the Checkerboard Block (page 68). Of course, if you'd rather use a different block—do it!

Unlike the other projects in this book, this bag mostly makes use of specific cut shapes instead of blocks. You can choose to piece the shapes from blocks or block scraps if you prefer. In the sample, only the Front Rounded Rectangle is pieced (using 2 HST Block scraps). Follow the Cutting Chart on the next page to cut the exterior, lining, batting, and binding needed for the bag.

Then, cut and piece 1 Checkerboard Block (page 68) and trim to a 9½″ × 11″ rectangle.

◖ HALF INCH BUFFER ◗

You'll notice that for each quilt sandwich, the lining fabric is 1″ wider and longer than the wool batting, which is 1″ wider and longer than the outside fabric. This gives a half inch buffer on every side of the outside fabric since fabric stretches during quilting.

FINISH PATTERN PIECES: Cutting Triangles

Stack the 4 squares 5″ × 5″ in a pile. Cut from one bottom corner to the center top of the squares. Repeat from the other bottom corner. This makes 4 triangles.

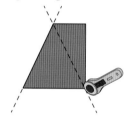

FINISH PATTERN PIECES: Trim Pocket

1. Along an 11″ edge of the Checkerboard Block, measure 5″ from the edge and mark. Repeat and mark 6½″ from the edge on a 9½″ side. Using a hera marker, draw a line between both marks that intersects the squares on a diagonal. Cut on the line.

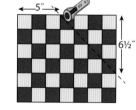

◖ FOLLOW THE DIAGONALS ◗

Sewing these Checkerboard Blocks is finicky business, and the dimensions of your Checkerboard Block might be off by a half an inch or so. For this first cut, line the ruler up with the diagonals of the checkerboard squares. That is more important than the exact distances noted above.

Continued on page 134.

CROSSBODY CUTTING CHART

Pattern Piece	Shape to Cut (and/or Piece)	Material and Color
Front Rectangle—exterior	9″ × 6½″ rectangle	Foxglove (X) Terra Cotta (T)
Front Rectangle—lining	10″ × 7½″ rectangle	Cinnamon (N)
Back Rectangle—exterior	9″ × 6½″ rectangle	Foxglove (X)
Back Rectangle—lining	10″ × 7½″ rectangle	Lingerie (G)
Front and Back Rectangles—batting	2 rectangles 10″ × 7½″	Batting
Pieced Pocket—lining	10″ × 5″ rectangle	Foxglove (X)
Pieced Pocket—batting	10″ × 5″ rectangle	Batting
Zipper Panel 1—exterior	2″ × 14½″ rectangle	Sage (S)
Zipper Panel 1—lining	3″ × 15½″ rectangle	Pickle (L)
Zipper Panel 2—exterior	2″ × 14½″ rectangle	Terra Cotta (T)
Zipper Panel 2—lining	3″ × 15½″ rectangle	Copen (D)
Zipper Panels—batting	2 rectangles 3″ × 15½″	Batting
Bottom Panel—exterior	3″ × 15¾″ rectangle	Pickle (L)
Bottom Panel—lining	4″ × 16¾″ rectangle	Sage (S)
Bottom Panel—batting	4″ × 16¾″ rectangle	Batting
Binding for Pocket	2½″ × 9″ rectangle	Pickle (L)
Binding for Zipper Panel 1	2½″ × 14½″ rectangle	Cantaloupe (II)
Binding for Zipper Panel 2	2½″ × 14½″ rectangle	Pickle (L)
Side Flaps exterior	4 squares 5″ × 5″; subcut into 4 triangles (see left)	Pink (K) Teal (E)
Interior Binding	2 strips 2½ × WOF	Lingerie (G)
Straps	1 piece 8″ and 1 piece 1¼ yards	Polypropylene webbing

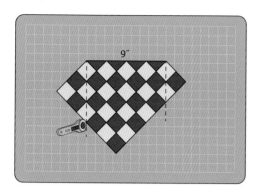

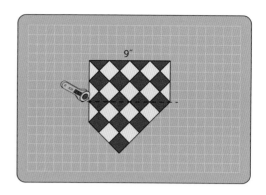

2. Turn the block so that the cut edge lines up with a horizontal line of the cutting mat. Using that edge as the top of the rectangle, trim the left and right sides of the block, leaving a 9″ length.

3. Measure 4″ down from the top edge and trim off the bottom, leaving a rectangle 9″ × 4.″

QUILTING THE SHAPES

Stack the exterior, batting, and lining layers by pattern piece to create 6 quilt sandwiches. Remember the lining fabric (the bottom of the sandwich) should be right side down and the outside fabric (the top of the sandwich) should be right side up. The 6 pattern pieces are: Front Rectangle, Back Rectangle, Pocket, Zipper Panel 1, Zipper Panel 2, Bottom Panel.

Pin baste each sandwich, and then quilt with a walking foot. You might quilt a grid, or on a diagonal, or in a cross hatch pattern. Use the hera marker and ruler as needed to make sure straight lines of stitching are precise.

Once all 6 quilt sandwiches are quilted, use the mat, ruler and rotary cutter to trim off the excess batting and lining fabric to make them the sizes listed for the exterior of each pattern piece in the Cutting Chart. Additionally, the pocket should measure 4″ × 9″, and you should have 4 Side Flap triangles.

ASSEMBLY

ADDING BINDING

Follow the instructions in Binding Pocket Edges (page 125) to bind a long side of the Zipper Panel 1, Zipper Panel 2, and Pocket quilt sandwiches.

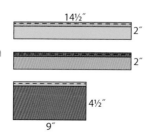

ROUNDING CORNERS AND POCKET ASSEMBLY

1. Stack the bound Pocket on top of the Front Rectangle (both right sides up), aligning the bottom edges. Sew around the 3 unbound edges of the pocket, attaching it to the Front Rectangle.

2. Using the Cross Body Bag Template, mark the 4 rounded corners. Cut the rounded corners.

3. Again using the Cross Body Bag Template, mark the 4 rounded corners on the Back Rectangle, too. Cut the rounded corners.

AFFIXING THE ZIPPER

1. Baste the bound edge of one zipper panel to one side of the zipper, with both sides facing up. You can use clips, or even a thin line of craft glue. With the walking foot, stitch the binding to the zipper, sewing ⅛″ away from the edge. The zipper should be underneath the binding.

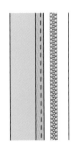

2. Repeat Step 1 to attach the second zipper panel to the other side of the zipper.

3. The total width of this new unit is dependent on the zipper, but is likely around 4″. Trim it down to 3″, measuring 1½″ from the center of the zipper to each side. Trim.

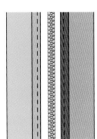

ASSEMBLING FLAPS

1. Measure 3″ from the base of the all 4 triangles, and mark a line.

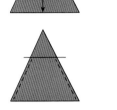

2. Stack and align 2 triangles of different colors, right sides together. Sew as shown, backstitching securely at the start and end. Repeat with the second pair. Turn the flaps right side out, pushing out the corners.

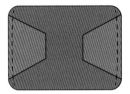

3. Place the Back Rounded Rectangle piece right side up. Pin the Step 2 units on the left and right of the panel as shown. Sew the base of each triangle to the Back Rounded Rectangle.

4. Using your fingers, push the unsewn tips of the triangles inside. Smooth out and Press.

▶ FINDING CENTERS

Finding the centers of the pieces is going to help keep the Cross Body Wonder Bag from getting wonky during assembly. With a ruler and water soluble pen, find and mark the center point of the Front Rectangle (and Pocket), Back Rectangle, Zipper Panel, and Bottom Panel.

FINAL ASSEMBLY

1. Unzip the zipper about 2˝. Align the left short sides of the Bottom Panel and Zipper Panel, right sides facing. Sew together along that side, moving slowly over the zipper.

2. Move the remaining short side of the Zipper Panel to match the right side of the Bottom Panel. Sew together along the second side, again moving slowly over the zipper. This creates a circle piece.

3. Place the Front Rectangle (pocket facing up) underneath the unit from Step 2, lining up the centers of both pieces. Pin or clip all the way around, making sure the centers of the pieces remain aligned. Using the walking foot and lots of patience, sew around the entire outside of the unit.

4. Repeat Steps 4–5 to attach the Back Rounded Rectangle to the bag.

5. Open the zipper the rest of the way. Turn the bag right side out and press out the corners.

BINDING SEAMS

Want to know a secret? When I make Cross Body Wonder Bags for myself, I never bind the inside seams. No one else sees them but me! And I *hate* binding inside seams. But if you wish to do this, follow the instructions in Interior Binding and Finishing (page 129) of the Get Going Duffle.

ADDING STRAPS AND BUCKLES

I will refer to the 2 parts of the side release buckle as the "shell" part (the part with the empty space inside) and the "crab" part (the part that goes inside the shell.)

1. Thread an end of the 8˝ strapping through the shell piece buckle and fold over. Gently ease both loose ends of the strapping inside one of the triangle flaps. Clip or pin in place.

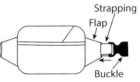

Strapping
Flap
Buckle

▎WHICH FLAPPY FLAP GETS THE SHELL? ▎

I like the shell part of the buckle to be on the right side of the bag (when I am looking at the bag.) But you can decide based on your handedness and preferences.

2. Using the walking foot, sew a line of stitching across the flap as shown. Backstitch, turn around, and stitch again. Then, sew a triangle.

Strap
Flap

3. Gently ease an end of the 1¼ yard length strapping into the open end of the other triangle flap. Repeat Step 2 to attach the strap.

4. Thread the tri-glide buckle onto the other end of the long strap, threading it over the center bar. Then, thread the strap through the crab part of the buckle. Finally, bring the end of the strap back through the tri-glide buckle as far as you can, back over the top of the center bar.

5. Fold the end of the strapping over about ¼.˝ Fold over another ¼.˝ Sew the end of the strap down with a zig zag stitch and the walking foot. Backstitch a couple times.

6. Adjust, pull, and wiggle the strap and tri-glide to get the Cross Body Wonder Bag to fit just how you like it. Trim any loose threads.

IMPROV TECHNIQUE 2 BAG
Make Room Market Tote

In Grand Rapids, we have an incredible farmer's market that sells everything from local eggs to organic popsicles to Michigan cherries. Everytime I think I'll just buy green beans, I end up walking back to my car with arms so full that by the time I get there, my blooms are crushed and my baguette is smushed. I thought to myself, "Self, you can make a bag for this," and I created a shallow, sturdy, wide-opening produce bag that makes room for just what I need. Share your makes with **#makeroommarkettote**

Materials

Yardages are based on 42" of usable width.

Kona cotton solid scraps (see below)

Backing: ⅔ yard

Lining: ½ yard

Binding: 2½" × 22"

1½" heavy polypropylene webbing (strapping): 2 yards

Batting (any kind): rectangle 21" × 34" (about 1 yard)

Market Tote Template (page 11)

Half-Circle Templates if sewing curved blocks (optional) (page 11)

CUTTING AND PIECING

For this project, we'll use several blocks from Technique 3: All the Colors, All the Shapes (page 64). The ones that I especially like to use when piecing the outside of the tote are the Checkerboard Block, Half-Square Triangle (HST) Block, Stripey Stripes Block, Half-Rectangle Triangle (HRT) Block, and Three Stripe Block.

Following instructions in Technique 3: All the Colors, All the Shapes (page 64), make 8–12 total blocks. Because the "quilt top" will be so much smaller, try out small variations of the blocks.

Then, using the tips for Assembling All the Blocks (page 75) sew your blocks together to make a mini quilt top around 17" × 30."

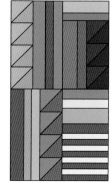

Market bag mini quilt

CHOOSING MATERIALS

Scrap fabrics are perfect for making the outside of the tote. Quilting cotton yardage, though, works well for the interior fabric and binding. Any type of batting works well for this project.

▶ **MAKING IT WATER-RESISTANT**

Here is a crazy idea: what if your market bag was water-resistant!? To enact that crazy idea, just use a water-resistant fabric instead of cotton for the lining fabric. See my thoughts about water-resistant fabrics in Choosing Water-Resistant Backing Fabric (page 90).

Using scrap fabrics for this project might feel constraining. If it adds more stress, you can always pull out fabric yardage and cut fresh pieces to make Technique 3 blocks. I want to encourage you, though, to stretch your creativity and ingenuity by using scrap fabrics.

For the sample Market Tote, I used scrap fabrics in colors: CC, D, H, II, JJ, K, O, P, Q, R, S, T, U, W, X. If you want to use yardage instead of scrap fabrics, a fat eighth of 10–12 colors will be enough.

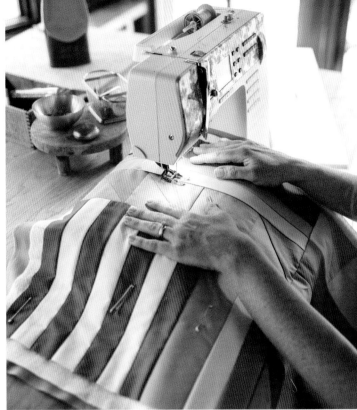

QUILTING THE TOTE EXTERIOR

Stack the Bag Exterior and batting (right side facing up). With the walking foot, quilt just those 2 layers as desired. Straight lines, a grid pattern, free motion or "stitch in the ditch" all work well for this project. Then trim the extra batting from the sides, making sure it measures 17″ × 30.″

Fold the Bag Exterior in half. Using the Market Tote Template, mark the rounded corners and cut them off. Stack the rounded unit on the lining fabric, unfolded. Mark the shape, then cut it out of the lining fabric.

ADDING STRAPS

1. Draw a line through the center of the Bag Exterior with a water-soluble marker. Mark a short line on each side, measuring 4″ 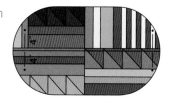 on either side of the center line. Cut the webbing into 2 strap lengths, each somewhere between 30″–33″, as you prefer. Make them both the same length.

2. Line up one of the straps on the 4″ marks on one short side. Pin or clip. Make sure the strap is not twisted. Align the edges of the straps with the edges of the bag, then sew with a walking foot.

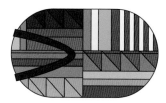

3. Repeat Step 2 with the second strap.

ASSEMBLING THE TOTE

1. Stack the Exterior and lining, right sides together. Pin all the way around. Sew together, leaving a 6″ unsewn gap on one side. Backstitch over the straps.

2. Turn the bag right side out through the gap, pushing out all the edges. Gently fold in the raw edges of the gap ½″, and press. Pin.

3. Sew along the entire oval again with the walking foot, topstitching with a ¼″ seam and closing the gap.

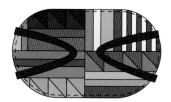

4. Fold the unit in half, exterior side facing in. Clip or pin around the curve. Measure 10″ up from the fold on both sides, and mark as shown. Sew the sides, from the 10″ marks to the fold. Backstitch at both ends.

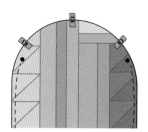

An example of another Market Tote improvised with scrap fabrics and made with 4″ extra length.

BIND THE SEAMS

1. Follow the instructions in Interior Binding and Finishing (page 129) to bind the 2 side seams. Turn the bag right side out.

About the Author

Laura Veenema is a born-and-raised Michigander, whose earliest memories involve creating–castles of sand in the summer and forts of snow in the winter. She had a particular penchant for quilts, though no one in her family sewed. At nine, she hand stitched a mini quilt for a school social studies project. At ten, she asked her parents to paint squares of color on her bedroom walls. At fourteen, she was appliquéing fleece blankets. But it wouldn't be until adulthood that she would learn to use a sewing machine.

Her professional career began as a middle-school teacher in Chicago where she moved with her husband, Jeremy. It was there that she earned a master's degree in Reading, had her first child, and learned how to sew—all in the same year! That year, a new song of joy started humming in her heart right in tune with her new sewing machine.

Laura was soon devoting every spare minute to quilting. She delighted in experimenting with new colors and designs, but disliked following other people's patterns, so she began to sketch out her own. Soon she started developing improvisational techniques that allowed her to rely on her own whims and creativity. Quilting—and specifically modern improv quilting—became a respite, a comfort, a great joy, and a little business: New Song Quilting Co.

Laura and Jeremy moved back home to Grand Rapids, Michigan and welcomed two more sons and a daughter. All the while, Laura was sharpening her improv quilting skills alongside raising a family and working as a literacy coach. In 2019, when their third son was just 11 months old, he was diagnosed with Type I Diabetes, a life-threatening and life-long condition that requires constant blood sugar management. To be able to care for him at home full-time, Laura transitioned away from educational work and poured herself into New Song Quilting Co.

In every new season, Laura's sewing machine keeps humming. She keeps creating. Through the New Song Quilting Co. website, she offers both pattern pdfs and physical quilted goods. Through her social media account, she delights in connecting with quilters around the globe. She treasures that community of quilters trying to pull Heaven down to earth, one modern quilt at a time.

And now, through this book, Laura offers her modern improvisational quilting ideas to anyone looking for a new song to sing. May these techniques and projects—and the joy and freedom of modern improv quilting—sing over everyone who reads it.